Wings of Yesteryear

The Golden Age of Private Aircraft

Geza Szurovy

MBI Publishing Company

First published in 1998 by MBI Publishing Company, 729 Prospect Avenue, PO Box 1, Osceola, WI 54020-0001 USA.

MBI Publishing Company books are also available at discounts in bulk quantity for industrial or sales-promotional use. For details write to Special Sales Manager at Motorbooks International Wholesalers & Distributors, 729 Prospect Avenue, PO Box 1, Osceola, WI, 54020-0001.

Photos by or via Geza Szurovy unless otherwise stated.

Library of Congress Cataloging-in-Publication Data Available.

Szurovy, Geza.
   Wings of yesteryear : the golden age of private aircraft / Geza Szurovy.
     p.   cm.
   Includes index.
   ISBN 0-7603-0397-5 (alk. paper)

1. Aeronautics--United States--History. 2. Private flying--United States History. 3. Private planes-- United States--History.
I. Title.
TL521.S98   1998
629.13'0973--dc21   98-14511

On the front cover: The first cabin Waco was the QDC, introduced in 1931. The QDC was based on the open-cockpit QDF's airframe. The fuselage was scaled up into an enclosed four-seat cabin. Power came from a 165-horsepower Continental. *Richard Vander Meulen*

On the frontispiece: Engine and aluminum skin warming in the rising sun, a Spartan Executive prepares for departure.

On the title page: A Spartan Executive (left) and Howard DGA (right) illustrate the rapid changes taking place in aircraft design.

On the back cover, top: The 1938 Cessna C-38 got a bow leg to increase the wheelbase, a belly flap, and was the first to be called the Airmaster, a name retroactively applied to the entire line. *Jim Koepnick/EAA*

On the back cover, bottom: An advertisement for Naturaline a brand of aviation gasoline. Oil companies were the first to grasp the importance of the personal-business airplane, not only as a lucrative market for their products, but also as efficient transportation through their far-flung territories.

Edited by Mike Haenggi
Designed by Katie L. Sonmor and Amy Huberty

Printed in Hong Kong through World Print, Ltd.

CONTENTS

ACKNOWLEDGMENTS

Thanks is due first and foremost to everyone who ever did anything to restore and keep an antique airplane flying. The dedicated efforts of the antique airplane community give all of us the gift of experiencing the past come alive.

Several organizations and their members were most helpful in providing photographs and other material and arranging generous photo opportunities. Jim Koepnick of the Experimental Aircraft Association made available some of the best photos he and his colleagues have taken over the years. Gene DeMarco of the Old Rhinebeck Aerodrome shared with me his big, beautiful Howard DGA, his feisty Stampe, and his sources of information. Mark Grusauski gave me the run of Wingworks at the lovely grass airfield in North Canaan, Connecticut, let me in on the trade secrets of the restorer, and arranged a date with Larry Smith's exquisite Spartan Executive. Bob and Brent Taylor welcomed me to the Antique Airplane Association's annual Labor Day fly-in in Blakesburg, Iowa, and introduced me to some of the rarest antiques still flying.

Thanks are also due to many others for being helpful in various ways over the years, including Al Buchner for letting us feature his lovely Waco QDC, which is on the cover, Brian Gall (Cub Coupe), Clifton Jaeger (Husky photo plane), Ritts Howard (Aeronca Champ), Sam Brunetto (Stearman PT-17), Ken Love (Matty Laird's original Laird), the Tiger Club of England, Bill King (Tiger Moth), Billy Copp (Globe Swift), Chris Siderwitz (Stinson Junior), Ed Wegner (Spartan C-3), Ted Davis (Taperwing Waco), Lee and Donna Parsons (Waco QCF), Bill Lumley (Aeronca C-3), Bob and Susie Reinauer (Cessna Airmaster), Bill Shires (Cessna 140), and photographers Richard Vander Meulen, Martin Berinstein, and Jim Williamson.

$\mathcal{I}$NTRODUCTION

Travel Air, Waco, Stinson Reliant, Staggerwing, Stearman, Ryan, Cub, Monocoupe . . . the names evoke an image of frolicking among cotton wool clouds on a long-gone summer afternoon. The years from the end of World War I until storm clouds once again darkened the horizon were an age of momentous technological progress for personal aviation, every bit as thrilling as the age of the personal computer is today. In a mere two decades personal aircraft performance expanded exponentially from the limited capabilities of the frail Curtiss Jenny to the 450-horsepower cabin-class Beech Staggerwing and its peers that could fly from New York to Los Angeles in a day.

When one looks back on that time, the barnstormers, the long distance record fliers, the air racers, and the world of air transportation and military aviation have traditionally claimed the lion's share of attention. Yet this was also the time when the personal airplane came into its own, flown for pleasure and business. It is this group of aircraft that most effectively brings those days alive through the efforts of the dedicated antique airplane buffs who lovingly restore them to original condition and fly them as they were flown in their heyday.

This book is the story of this special group of airplanes, not only as it can be garnered from the black and white period photos, the memorabilia, and the history books, but also as it can be experienced by going out to any number of airports throughout the country and seeing them in action. There is no better way to understand what they were all about than by watching them in living color as they thunder into the air from an ageless grass strip or by flying them whenever the opportunity arises.

As the limits of airframe and engine technology were conquered, these aircraft rapidly progressed beyond the simple, open-cockpit biplanes, such as the Travel Airs, the early Wacos, and Lairds. After the shock of the Great Depression, they reached their zenith in such extravagant art deco cabin-class creations as the Beech Staggerwing, the Cabin Wacos, the Stinson Reliant, and the Spartan Executive, all propelled by massively powerful radial engines.

They were eased out of their predominant role by the appearance of much smaller, lighter, and less expensive engines that made the radials and the aircraft they powered obsolete and democratized personal aviation into a widely affordable passion. But the grand old airplanes didn't just fade away. As cherished antiques they continue to bring us the excitement of an epic time that otherwise most of us would never know.

Free To Fly

The frail Bleriot-type monoplane named *Silverwing* trundled erratically down the plowed, soft wheat field south of Enid, Oklahoma. Its chattering four-cylinder Elbridge engine blew a steady plume of oily soot right into the pilot's goggled face. After a ground roll of about 300 feet, it was suddenly airborne and began a laborious, shallow climb into the light east wind.

At around 200 feet the pilot manipulated *Silverwing's* wing warping mechanism to turn downwind. A modest gathering of Enid's citizens watched, awestruck, as the rag-winged kite sailed gracefully overhead. They became increasingly exuberant as it turned back toward the field and the pilot cut the ignition on short final. Now all they could hear in the silence of the winter chill was the wind whistling softly in the maze of flying wires as *Silverwing* descended to a perfect landing.

Few in the crowd who swarmed around the airplane realized that the pilot was the most jubilant of them all. He was Clyde Cessna and he had good reason to celebrate. After a year of hops, false starts, and crashes that could have killed him, he had at last succeeded in truly flying—taking off, making turns, remaining airborne for more than seven minutes, and landing back in one piece where he had taken off. It was December 17, 1911, eight years to the day after Orville Wright's historic 98-second hop at Kitty Hawk.

Cessna's flight didn't set the telegraph wires on fire or make the front page of the *New York Times*. Others were capturing the limelight with far more impressive flights by then, but his little-noticed jaunt around the patch was one of the first achievements by a new breed of up-and-coming aviators who would establish the foundations of personal and corporate aviation.

Cessna's path to his private milestone in that Oklahoma wheat field reveals the individualism, tenacity, and entrepreneurial optimism that would drive him and his fellow pioneers to overcome the daunting obstacles hindering the development of any commercially successful aviation venture in the early years.

Clyde Cessna was a son of Kansas homesteaders. Although he had only a fifth-grade education, he was forever tinkering with the machinery on the farm and became a skilled self-taught mechanic by the time he grew up and began farming his own 40 acres near the family homestead. A purchase of a one-cylinder 4-horsepower car by his brother, Roy, got Clyde so hooked on horseless transportation that he gave up farming to become a salesman for an Overland car dealership. His success as a car salesman led to a move in 1908 to Enid, Oklahoma, where he became partner and general manager of the Cessna Automobile Company.

While he spent most of his time promoting the many virtues of the Overlands and the sporty new Clark roadsters he was selling, he also followed with keen interest the exploits of those pioneering dare-

The flight of this replica *Silverwing* accurately represents Clyde Cessna's first successful flight in his Bleriot derivative. He crashed several times while he taught himself to fly. The tricky wing-warping mechanism used by the Bleriot design that preceded ailerons didn't make his task easier. The lack of a reliable engine also plagued his early efforts. The Elbridge Aero engine was eventually replaced by a 60-horsepower Anzani radial, which proved to be acceptable. Cessna was a proto-barnstormer, flying for a fee at various gatherings to recoup the costs of his flying.
James H. Williamson

Clyde Cessna flying *Silverwing* outside Enid, Oklahoma, a few months after his first successful flight. On this flight *Silverwing* was still powered by the Elbridge engine. *National Air and Space Museum*

devils in their flying machines. He was particularly impressed by Louis Bleriot's crossing of the English Channel in 1909, a feat that captured the popular imagination as much as Lindbergh's transatlantic crossing would in a later time.

In January 1911 Cessna got to see the Bleriot mystique firsthand, when three French aviators flying Bleriot monoplanes held an aerial display over Oklahoma City. He was so taken that he decided on the spot he wanted nothing more than to fly his own Bleriot, the sooner the better. Within a month he was on the train to New York City and the Queen Aeroplane Company.

Back in those days it suited American business to be much less squeamish about licensing agreements and copyright concerns, and the Queen Aeroplane Company, owned by stockbroker Willis McCormick, was one of several places to go if you wanted a Bleriot monoplane without having to bother with the added expense of a stiff licensing fee paid to Monsieur Bleriot. The Queen Aeroplane Company was in the merry business of churning out knock-off Bleriots.

Clyde Cessna was welcomed with open arms, allowed to work on the assembly line for three weeks, and taken by company pilots on the first flight of his life. It thrilled him to no end, prompting him to make additional flights while at the factory and strengthening his resolve to fly his own pirated Bleriot. The Queen Aeroplane Company had just the airplane. It was a model that had been under construction for the well-known French-trained American exhibition pilot, John Moisant, when he crashed to his death in another Bleriot Type XI on a practice flight in New Orleans. Christened *Silverwing*, the unfinished airplane was completed, sold to Clyde Cessna for $7,500, and put on a train to Enid, Oklahoma.

When *Silverwing* was uncrated and assembled, Cessna set out with the typical "grab the bull by the horns" attitude of his time to teach himself to fly. The factory-supplied V-8 proved to be troublesome, developing only 30 horsepower instead of the promised 80

and was swapped for a 60-horsepower Elbridge Aero Special. Built by the Elbridge Engine Company of Rochester, New York, which had just branched out into aircraft engines beyond its traditional line of marine powerplants, it also had its problems with reliability but was at least powerful enough to get *Silverwing* airborne when it chose to run.

The summer of 1911 found Clyde Cessna encamped on the Great Salt Plains of Oklahoma near a town with the improbable name of Jet, performing increasingly ambitious hops in his airplane—interrupted by regular crashes followed by periods of reconstruction that gave him valuable experience in aircraft-building techniques. To recoup his not inconsiderable expenses, he optimistically booked demonstration hops at the various fairs in the nearby towns throughout the summer and early fall, which were all canceled for one reason or another and began to call into question his credibility.

By September 1911 he was a sufficiently competent pilot to make shallow turns when near disaster struck. He spun in from 60 feet, demolishing *Silverwing*, and was lucky to escape with his life. The results of the full rebuild that included tinkering with the engine to soup up its performance were promising. Cessna became increasingly comfortable handling the airplane and felt the day was close when he would have full control over it throughout an entire flight. Following one more serious crash, which broke the right wing, *Silverwing* was repaired yet again and relocated to the outskirts of Enid, where Cessna's dogged perseverance finally paid off on the eighth anniversary of Orville Wright's first flight.

Clyde Cessna made rapid progress after his first fully successful flight. His reputation as a local aviator soared along with *Silverwing* as he began delivering on his promises of exhibition flights and earning the fees he sought. He soon built the first airplane of his own design, an improved version of *Silverwing*, and earned enough from his exhibition flying to replace the cranky Elbridge with a coveted 60-horsepower Anzani radial engine. By the summer of 1914 he was measuring his flights not only in minutes, but hours as he routinely flew cross-country from site to site between his performances.

As Cessna flexed his wings over the prairie, others who would play important roles in the development of the personal airplane were also taking their first tentative steps into the fledgling world of aviation. Few among them found the kind of family inspiration that got Edward Stinson hooked. Eddie Stinson became infatuated with aviation in large measure because of his flying sisters, Katherine and Marjorie.

A Better Jenny?

The Jenny was one of the first mass-produced airplanes. More than 8,000 of the trainers were built for World War I service. It is little known that there was another trainer quite similar to the Jenny, and considered by many contemporary pilots to be a marginally better airplane. It was the Standard J-1.

The Standard was built by a New York company about two years after the Jenny's debut for the same purpose, so there was ample opportunity to tweak the Jenny concept. The Standard was reputed to handle more crisply and, unlike the Jenny, had a slightly swept wing. The early ones, although tail draggers, also had a weird, rather large nose wheel to prevent students from nosing over. Otherwise the two airplanes were practically identical. By all accounts the Standard should have claimed a big share of the more than 8,000 military orders for this type of trainer.

Its downfall was its engine, an obscure four-cylinder 100-horsepower Hall-Scott, which proved to be notoriously unreliable. In-flight fires were only one of its many hazards. So why wasn't the Standard equipped with the OX-5? Because the OX-5 was made by its competitor, Curtiss, which was putting them in its Jennies as fast as it could make them. Nevertheless, the Standard did get a chance, in spite of its engine. When the United States entered the war the military ordered about 1,600 Standards; however, in 1918 it took the unprecedented step of grounding the entire fleet because the Hall-Scotts were causing so many accidents.

Re-equipping the military Standards with the OX-5 was considered but rejected because it would have required fairly involved structural modifications of the engine mounts. It was simpler to order more Jennies. After the war there was more time to install OX-5s and Hissos in the surplus Standards, and many of them went on to a distinguished barnstorming career.

Katherine Stinson was the first in the family to get the flying bug. In the summer of 1911, when Clyde Cessna was experimenting with how badly he could scare himself in *Silverwing*, Katherine Stinson won a spot on a balloon flight over Kansas City. She was one of four women whose names were drawn from among more than 250 entrants. By the time the balloon touched down Katherine had vowed to learn to fly.

Making such a vow was easy for a young woman of 19 in those late Victorian days. The big challenge was overcoming the social obstacles to keep it. Katherine Stinson was lucky to have a formidable ally—her mother, Emma. Emma Stinson had a romantic sense for adventure and an independent mind that led her to encourage her children to pursue any serious interest regardless of social harrumphing to the contrary. She helped Katherine sell her piano for $200 and also convinced her tolerant husband to give their daughter the additional $300 required for a full course of flight instruction. She then vigorously lobbied any reputable flight instructor she came across to teach Katherine to fly.

Their efforts paid off when Katherine gained an introduction to Max Lillie, an agreeable and energetic flying instructor based at Cicero Field in Chicago. She started her flying lessons with him in a Wright Flyer B in the summer of 1912. Katherine proved to be such a natural pilot that after only four hours and ten minutes of dual she soloed, and three days later she became the fourth American woman to earn the prestigious Federation Aeronautique Internationale's (FAI) pilot's certificate.

The following spring Katherine and her mother formed the Stinson Aviation Company. She took the exhibition circuit by storm, performing from Ohio to Montana and all the way down through Texas to the Mexican border. A slight, vivacious woman, she was only 21 years old and looked even younger, never ceasing to startle the crowds who were much more accustomed to the macho pilot look.

Two years later, after Katherine became a pilot, her 19-year-old sister, Marjorie, also passed her FAI pilot's

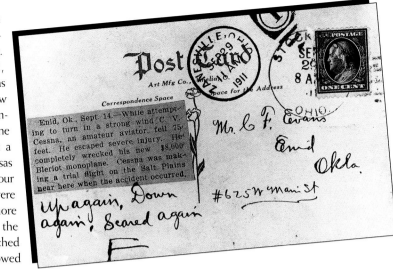

Clyde Cessna's road to success was arduous and physically dangerous. This postcard to a friend and early financial backer relating his last big crash before his successful first flight is revealing of his spirit. *National Air and Space Museum*

The Curtiss JN-4 Jenny was the ancestor of all American personal and business airplanes. More than 8,000 of these trainers were built for World War I. After the war they flooded the civilian market and became the staple aircraft of the barnstormers. The need for a more capable Jenny to take personal aviation beyond barnstorming led to the development of the early postwar three-seat biplanes, the first of which was the Laird Swallow.

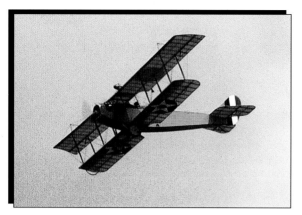

An impeccable formation of military JN-4 Jennies over some U.S. training fields in World War I. Eddie Stinson and Buck Weaver were Jenny instructors for the military. Sergeant Walter Beech worked on them as a mechanic. *National Air and Space Museum*

certificate requirements with flying colors and became an exhibition pilot in her own right. Their brother, Eddie, worked for them as their personal mechanic and was chafing at the bit to fly himself. In the fall of 1915 he decided to invest his modest savings in flying lessons at the Wright School of Flying in Dayton, Ohio. Although he didn't have enough resources to qualify for his FAI certificate he had become a competent pilot by the time he left to rejoin his sisters.

Eddie shared his sisters' natural talents for handling an airplane. Shortly after his stint at the Wright School he was flying the family Wright Flyer near San Antonio, Texas, where the Stinsons were wintering, when an elevator hinge bolt broke. Thinking fast, Eddie trimmed the airplane by shifting his weight around (a technique that was a desperate last-ditch effort by Stinson to save his life, but is used today for flying some hang gliders) and managed an emergency landing in, of all places, a cemetery. Stinson didn't relish the prospect of dismantling the Flyer and transporting it back to the airport overland, so he and the

cemetery attendant looked around and found a coffin bolt that was the right size. Eddie installed it and flew home.

It is worth noting that in those days you didn't need a pilot's certificate to be a pilot, nor were there any government airworthiness requirements. It was assumed, perhaps naively, that the self-preservation instinct was sufficient to control excessive risk taking. While this may seem rash, the airplanes of the era weren't that much different from today's ultralights, for which no pilot's certificate is required for flying solo in the United States, a policy supported by the reasonable accident statistics.

At Cicero Field, Eddie Stinson shared lodgings with another young aviation addict who would soon become a leading figure in the industry. He was Emil Matthew Laird, universally known as Matty. Laird became an avid model airplane builder while he was growing up. In 1913, with his brother, Charles, he decided to build a model big enough to fit his wiry little frame. He equipped it with a 15-horsepower home-built engine, dubbed it the Baby Biplane, and taught himself to fly in it. Laird was one of those rare, gifted individuals whose engineering and flying talents came easily.

The Baby Biplane flew well and other models followed, including the Bone Shaker. By 1915 Laird was able to earn reasonable performance fees to subsidize his design activities and build aircraft for use by others, including a Laird "looper" flown by Katherine Stinson.

Another close friend of Matty Laird and Eddie Stinson at Cicero Field was George "Buck" Weaver. Barely out of high school, he was a superb pilot and assisted Laird's airplane-building projects with great enthusiasm. Two of Weaver's close friends, Clayton Bruckner and Sam Yunkin, went to Buffalo, New York, around this time to join the Curtiss Aeroplane Company as apprentices. The three of them went on to start the Weaver Aircraft Company, better known to everyone who ever loved a biplane as Waco.

While Cessna, Laird, Stinson, Weaver, and others were making their way in the brave new world of flight, there appeared on the scene a flying machine that would play a pivotal role in all of their lives and would lay the foundation of the personal aviation industry. It was an open-cockpit two-seat biplane, the Curtiss Jenny, equipped with the OX-5 engine. As would often be the case with technical advances in aviation in the coming years, it owed its destiny to war.

World War I was the debut of the airplane as an indispensable instrument of war. By 1916 there was an increasing sense that the United States may be drawn into Europe's war, an adventure for which its military was ill prepared. Among the many shortcomings of America's peacetime army was the lack of an effective mass-produced primary

training airplane. As early as 1914 the Army had been looking for a new trainer, not because of the war in Europe, but because its pushers had the nasty habit of felling their pilots when the aft-mounted engines came loose in a crash.

The chief contender for becoming the military's new trainer with the engine up front (in "tractor" configuration, as it was then called) was a creation of the Curtiss Aeroplane Company, the Model J. It is less known that the design was the work of an English aeronautical engineer, B. Douglas Thomas, who was working for Sopwith Aviation Company at the time and had also worked for Vickers. Glenn Curtiss met him on a visit to England and talked him into designing the Model J, which he completed during the winter of 1913–1914.

To say that aircraft design was an imperfect science at the time is an understatement (spin recovery was yet to be understood), and the development of the Model J was no exception to this state of affairs. A lot of trial and error revealed many weaknesses of the Model J prototype, and in spite of a substantial increase in wing area that was incorporated following the initial test flights, it proved unacceptable to the Army. Thomas was asked to essentially redesign the airplane, which would be designated the Model N. But to save time, it was agreed that he would retain the fuselage of the J and design new wings. The new airplane was called the JN and was quickly nicknamed the Jenny.

The JN series proved more promising, and during 1915 and the summer of 1916 the trainer was refined into the JN4-A of which the Army promptly ordered a batch of 20. The Jenny was on its way. The big break for Curtiss came in April 1917 with the entry of the United States into World War I. Within days of the declaration of war Curtiss received an initial order for 600 JN4-As.

These early Jennies were further refined based on field experience. The airframe was strengthened by various small structural modifications. The engine's dihedral was reduced. The upper and lower wings' trailing edges in the cockpit area incorporated cutouts to improve the pilot's visibility. The control wheels that looked like car steering wheels and were in fairly common use in the early days were replaced by more practical control sticks. The final model designation was the JN4-D, which the Army wanted by the thousands.

Curtiss couldn't handle the production demands alone. In a practice that was to become common in World War II when the Ford Motor Company built a B-24 Liberator every four hours, the Jenny's production was farmed out to subcontractors. A version known as the Canuck was built in Canada. Altogether some 8,000 Jennies were built in the year and a half that remained until Armistice Day, and when the war

was over they came flooding onto the civilian market. The wild frenzy of barnstorming they sparked did more to popularize aviation than the most expensive public relations campaign could have ever done. They also set the standard that aspiring manufacturers of personal airplanes would have to surpass to succeed.

Curtiss made another vital contribution to the progress of personal aviation with the Jenny that reached well beyond the type. It was the trainer's engine, the 90-horsepower OX-5. A sufficient and reliable source of power was one of the biggest challenges facing airplane designers once basic airframe concepts were understood. Because of technological limitations, the power-to-weight ratio of engines was very low. In the pre-World War I era an aircraft engine that could produce 40 to 60 horsepower was considered high performance, yet its weight seriously limited the weight available for the airframe and payload to achieve sustained flight.

Pushing against the limits of the day's technology also caused reliability problems. Engine failures were endemic as engine components failed and fuel systems

This close-up of the Curtiss JN-4 Jenny shows the maze of bracing wires necessary for the wings' structural integrity. The wires were very useful to the wing walkers who had something to hold onto as they scrambled all over the airframe. The OX-5 liquid-cooled V-8 engine is also visible. Note the radiator cap. More than 12,000 OX-5s were made, most during World War I. The OX-5 was a standard engine through the 1920s biplane era, available by the late 1920s for as little as $250.

The irrepressible Hollywood stunt pilot Art Goebel maneuvers to enable the wing walker to make the hair-raising midair transfer from one Jenny to another. *National Air and Space Museum*

What open cockpit is all about. Bill King's Tiger Moth appeared a decade and a half after the Jenny, but the experience is the same. The Moth's empennage is especially reminiscent of the Jenny in appearance. *Martin Berinstein*

malfunctioned. Pistons, crankshafts, and other parts wore out in a relatively few hours of flight time, necessitating frequent overhauls. Cooling proved to be a major challenge. Liquid-cooled engines tended to be too heavy while effective air cooling proved difficult to achieve.

The Curtiss Aeroplane Company faced these challenges in-house. Unlike most aircraft makers, who from the earliest days have purchased the engines for their designs from companies specializing in engine manufacturing, Curtiss was an engine maker in its own right. Glenn Curtiss first made his mark racing bicycles and motorcycles, an experience that led him into a venture manufacturing small, air-cooled engines. He then went to work for Alexander Graham Bell's Aerial Experiment Association where his responsibility was engine development. By the time he left in 1909 he concluded that because of the difficulties he encountered with air cooling, a water-cooled V-8 was the best bet for an aircraft engine of reasonable power, weight, and reliability.

Curtiss unveiled his V-8 in 1912, calling it the Model O. It proved to have valve problems, which required a redesign that was completed by 1913. According to some historians, the intention was to call the improved engine the O-Plus, but a misaligned plus sign forever dubbed it the OX. It went through incremental improvements, and in 1917 its final version, the OX-5, was specified for the mass-produced Jennies. It was rated at 90 horsepower at 1,400 rpm and weighed 450 pounds. While it aquired an enduring reputation for being unreliable, if properly operated and maintained, it would run as long as 300 hours before requiring a top overhaul and up to 700 hours to a major overhaul.

The OX-5 was produced by the thousands during the final year and a half of World War I, not only for the Jennies but other aircraft in its class. Like the Jennies, it was also made by subcontractors in addition to Curtiss. It is estimat-

ed that by war's end more than 12,000 OX-5s had been manufactured. The builders of personal aircraft in the immediate postwar era did not have far to look for an engine.

In the meantime, the Great War was providing a variety of opportunities for the future pioneers of personal aviation to hone their flying skills. When the war broke out America's flight training capability was minimal, Canada's nonexistent. The U.S. military began sending a handful of officers to civilian flight schools, and scores of young Canadians eager to join the fray in the skies over Europe were looking for flight instruction. By late 1915 the astute Mrs. Stinson decided the time had come to establish a flying school.

The Stinsons' flying school in San Antonio, Texas, was run primarily by Marjorie (while Katherine continued to concentrate on exhibition flying, including a wildly successful tour of Japan and China, for which she borrowed a looper from Matty Laird). The majority of Marjorie's students were Canadians, the first five of whom qualified for their FAI pilot's certificates in December 1915, along with Eddie Stinson who was one of the school's mechanics. The first batch of graduates (minus Eddie) went on to fly as commissioned officers in the Royal Naval Air Service.

By the end of 1917, when several U.S. military flight training centers were up and running and the government closed down all civilian flying to save resources for the war effort, Marjorie Stinson personally had trained 83 Canadian pilots who went on to fly in World War I.

It was the war that gave Eddie Stinson his big opportunity to fly full time instead of remaining his sisters' mechanic. In late 1916 the U.S. Army mounted a massive effort to build up its aviation capability, and Eddie was asked to join as a civilian flight instructor. Three days after America entered the war he led a flight of four Jennies into a vast, windswept dirt field outside San Antonio. He was the first to touch down at the Army's newest training facility, Kelly Field, whose name would be so prominently linked not to one, but two world wars.

At Kelly Field and other training bases where he served, Stinson became a legend for his aerobatic skills. He also performed occasional flight testing for Curtiss, and by war's end he had matured into one of the most experienced pilots in the country.

Buck Weaver also became a civilian flight instructor for the military, flying out of Rich Field in Waco, Texas. Serving at the same base was a sergeant and former auto mechanic in his late 20s, in charge of engine maintenance—Walter H. Beech. According to his own accounts, his first brush with flying was in 1914 when he restored a crashed Curtiss pusher and, in the manner of the day, proceeded to teach himself the basics of flying. But the war put any chance of flying on hold as Beech looked after the OX-5s, Hispano Suizas, and Liberty engines that powered the fleet at Rich Field.

The war also gave Lloyd Stearman and Don Luscombe their first brush with flying. Stearman saw his first airplane in Harper, Kansas, when he attended a flight demonstration put on by none other than Clyde Cessna. Prompted in part by the experience, he signed up for naval flight training near the end of the war. He entered the program too late to make any substantial progress, but was sufficiently bitten by the flying bug to keep an aviation career in the back of his mind in spite of becoming an architect.

When America entered World War I, Don Luscombe interrupted his college studies at the University of Iowa to volunteer as a driver in the Ambulance Corps in France. There he became friendly with the pilots of a French flying unit based in his sector. It wasn't long before he convinced them with his born salesman's flair to take him for his first airplane ride in a Voisin biplane. The Voisin was a pusher in which the observer sat in front of the pilot in an enclosure reminiscent of an open pulpit—with the best view in France. Luscombe was thrilled by the experience and went along on subsequent flights whenever he could. When he returned to the United States after the war he did the responsible thing and went into advertising, but it wasn't long before he returned to flying.

Meanwhile, in late 1916 Clyde Cessna was approached by a group of businessmen from Wichita, Kansas, who wanted their town to get a head start in playing a role in aviation. They wanted Cessna to produce his monoplanes in Wichita and set up a flying school. They offered space in the Jones automobile factory and Cessna accepted. And so it happened that the first airplane to be built in Wichita was a Cessna. It was a further improvement on the Bleriot design and made its maiden flight within a few months after Cessna moved to town.

In the summer of 1917 Cessna opened the flying school, with three students to be trained in the airplane he built in 1913. He also continued working feverishly on his next design, a two-place version of his latest creation. Powered by a new 60-horsepower Anzani, it flew in July 1917 and so impressed its creator that he named it *Comet*. Its most visible advanced feature was a streamlined nose in which one could faintly recognize the beginnings of the lines that would characterize Cessna's enclosed cabin designs.

Cessna was hopeful that he would get a military contract for building the *Comet* and training pilots in it for the Army. But by then the government had established its own Jenny-equipped primary training centers and had, in fact, decided to prohibit all civilian flying in the interest of the war effort. After successfully teaching one of his students to fly, Clyde Cessna returned to farming in Rago, Kansas, for the time being, seeing it as the best contribution he could now make to the war.

By the time Armistice Day dawned on November 11, 1918, a greater number of Americans were itching to make a living out of aviation than ever before. They had at their disposal a vast fleet of bargain-priced surplus Jennies to barnstorm across America and transform it into the most air-minded nation in the world. And such entrepreneurs as Laird, Cessna, Beech, Stearman, Stinson, and Luscombe would make owning an airplane no different than owning the family car or corporate limo.

Matty Laird (right) with his first successful airplane, the 12-horsepower Baby Tractor Biplane. Laird, an avid model builder, took the novel approach of scaling up his successful models until he could fit in one. *National Air and Space Museum*

The flying Stinson sisters. Katherine (right) was the fourth U.S. woman to be awarded her pilot's license when she met all the requirements in July 1912. Her sister, Marjorie, followed two years later. Katherine had a spectacular air show career while Marjorie trained Canadian pilots for World War I. Their younger brother, Eddie, was a pioneer of the concept of the enclosed-cockpit personal airplane. *National Air and Space Museum*

CHAPTER 2

LEAPS OF FAITH

The flying circus of Jennies and Standards that stormed across America in the aftermath of World War I titillated the crowds, frolicking above them as daredevils hung from the landing gear struts and played tennis on the wings. For a dollar or two they gave the first glimpse of the world from a bird's-eye view to thousands who were born before there were even cars, let alone airplanes. They were masters at sowing the seeds of our romance with the air, but if aviation was to progress beyond the flying circus, new, more capable designs were needed, along with the capital to build them. Slowly this notion gained recognition.

Some of the more technically inclined barnstormers and imaginative tinkerers and engineers dreamed of designing their own airplanes that would be superior to the war-surplus crates and were beginning to sketch out their ideas in their spare moments. And a small but growing number of businessmen were beginning to think that aviation had a commercial future in which there was money to be made.

It required a gambler's appetite for risk to stake money on aviation, and among the entrepreneurs most likely to understand what they would be getting into were the oil men. The oil industry was in a wild, free-for-all boom of its own, not all that different from the barnstormer's world. Wildcatters (as the drillers were called) understood the odds. They could lose their shirts on a hundred dry holes before they struck a gusher that would make them rich, and there was a good chance that they never would.

The oil men also had a need to make their way around their concessions as efficiently as possible in some of the most inaccessible terrain in the country. They quickly grasped the potential of making their rounds in a company airplane. When they found that the available airplanes were not up to the task, rather than forget about them, their "can-do" approach to life tended to make them wonder why someone doesn't build an airplane that could do the job. Oil men were prominent early supporters of personal and company airplanes and were among the best customers for them when they became available. Some went even further. They got directly into the airplane business.

One such oil man was Jacob Melvin Moellendick, a wildcatter based in Wichita, Kansas, who had struck his share of gushers. More optimistic than most, Jake Moellendick started the Wichita Airplane Company in 1919 with a fleet of two war surplus Jennies. It was to be an air taxi service that would also provide flight instruction and rides. But the business wasn't going anywhere and Moellendick realized it was because the Jennies weren't sufficiently capable. They were good enough for entertainment and to teach someone to fly, but they weren't transportation and earned little from

The Travel Air was designed by Lloyd Stearman in 1924–1925. It had a steel tube fuselage, a concept Walter Beech and Stearman first offered to their boss, Jake Moellendick, at the Swallow Airplane Manufacturing Company. When Moellendick rebuffed them, the two quit, joined forces with Clyde Cessna, and formed Travel Air. Note the "elephant ear" formed by the aerodynamically balanced aileron. The elephant ear and the rudder shape show the influence of Anthony Fokker's World War I D-VII fighter on Stearman. Pictured is a Wright-powered Travel Air 4000. The first Travel Air was the OX-5-powered Model A. Later designated the 2000, it was Travel Air's low-cost model for some years.

Matty Laird in the Laird Swallow, the design he derived from the Curtiss Jenny. Financed by oil man Jake Moellendick, the Swallow laid the foundation of the personal airplane industry in Wichita, Kansas, in 1920. *National Air and Space Museum*

Walter Beech (right) and Lloyd Stearman, standing next to two sparkling New Swallows, review on a chart the route they plan to fly to Dayton, Ohio, from Wichita, Kansas, circa 1924. The Stearman-designed New Swallow represented a significant aerodynamic improvement over Laird's original Swallow design. It retained the wood-and-fabric fuselage. When Jake Moellendick vetoed Stearman's and Beech's proposal to build an improved version with a steel tube fuselage frame, the two left to establish Travel Air and realize their plans. *National Air and Space Museum*

now he proudly showed off the plans for the new three-place airplane. As it turned out, Burke became a friend of Jake Moellendick, the man with capital in search of an airplane. Burke, now living in Wichita himself, played matchmaker and the deal was struck. Wichita was to be the home of the new E. M. Laird Airplane Company, a partnership between Moellendick, Laird, and Burke.

Matty Laird moved to Wichita in early 1920 and by April he was at the controls himself on his new design's maiden flight. Someone always feels compelled to blurt out something at such events instead of

one-passenger-at-a-time joyrides. To earn a reasonable return a new design was required, one that could carry more than one passenger.

That was also the view of Matty Laird who had moved his base of operations from Chicago's Cicero Field when it closed to nearby Ashburn Field, the new home of the Aero Club of Illinois. As a barnstormer Laird saw a doubling of ride revenue per flight if he could only stuff two passengers into his Jenny instead of one. It was too tempting an idea to just keep thinking about it, so Laird designed the airplane he had in mind.

It was essentially a modified three-place Jenny. The pilot was still alone in the rear cockpit, but up front there was room for two passengers side by side on a bench seat. The engine was the OX-5, the wings were still double bay (supported by two sets of struts each), and construction was wood and fabric, just like the Jenny. All Laird needed now to build his airplane was capital. Raising money was the toughest challenge for the destitute designers of the day, but Laird lucked out.

He ran across an old acquaintance named William Burke, who was a part-time flying circus promoter. Matty had sold Burke one of his earlier designs and

just watching the show, and on this occasion the memorable phrase was "there she goes boys, just like a swallow." The Laird Swallow it was.

The Laird Airplane Company sold four Swallows in the first year, in spite of a price that had to be set well above the going rate for the war-surplus machines because of production costs. The extra seat was attracting buyers. The sales volume was sufficient to justify hiring an assistant to Matty Laird.

From among the few respondents to an advertisement in the local Wichita paper Laird chose Lloyd Stearman, who had completed his education after leaving the Naval air cadet program and was working as an architect. Stearman had never lost sight of his dream to work with airplanes. He didn't get to do design assignments right away, though. As was the custom in those days, he was put to work on the shop floor building airframe components to learn the business from the bottom up.

While the Laird Airplane Company was getting organized in Wichita, Clayt Bruckner and Sam Yunkin, the two aspiring airplane designers who started on the shop floor at Curtiss, were leaving Buffalo,

New York. They were headed down along the shore of Lake Erie to Lorain, Ohio, for a reunion with their friend Buck Weaver.

Following the end of the war Weaver got together with another flight instructor, Charlie Meyers, and they went on the barnstorming trail with two Canucks. As the business prospered they added two more Canucks and three pilots and based themselves in Lorain, where they established the Ohio Aviation School and continued their regional barnstorming activities. Bruckner and Yunkin joined the group here as mechanics and wingwalkers, but their primary objective was to revive the plans they had with Weaver to get into the airplane-making business.

Bruckner and Yunkin had dabbled with a couple of unsuccessful flivver designs (today they would be called ultralights), one a flying boat, while progressing to the position of quality control inspectors at Curtiss and working as draftsmen at Aeromarine in New Jersey. Now, with the support of Weaver, they embarked on designing yet another flivver. It was to be a tiny parasolwinged wood-and-fabric airplane called the *Cootie*, powered by a 28-horsepower two-cylinder air-cooled engine. When the *Cootie* plans solidified, Weaver, Bruckner, and Yunkin decided to incorporate as the Weaver Aircraft Company, or Waco for short.

The origin of the name Waco has caused some confusion. Logically it is a convenient abbreviation of Weaver Aircraft Company. It is often said that it has nothing to do with Waco, Texas, and Weaver's tenure there as an Army flight instructor at Rich Field. It is, however, true that the Army's Rich Field battle cry was "HOO-AAH-KO!" (which they often spelled in unit newsletters as WAAA-CO). It became a favorite yell of Weaver's, which he used frequently long after his Rich Field days, especially in the company of former Army flyers. Whether his idea for the company name came first, or was influenced by the battle cry, we'll never know.

The Weaver Aircraft Company optimistically advertised the Cootie Parasol Monoplane in the aviation press for the bargain price of $1,200. Buck Weaver flew it for the first time in early 1920 and promptly totaled it on landing, blinded at the last moment by a sneaky swirl of ground fog. A setback to be sure, but at last a Yunkin-Bruckner design had flown.

It was back to the drawing board and the result was *Cootie 2*, a biplane version of its predecessor with the same engine. The company attempted to raise stock to fund it. The effort turned out to be a spectacular failure. Weaver saw little immediate chance for any serious income from the Waco venture and was in a personal bind. He had a family to support. When his

ABOVE LEFT: Walter Beech flying a Travel Air Model A. Note the characteristic boxy shape given the airplane's nose by the cowled OX-5. Also, note the aileron pushrods aft of the wing struts, an arrangement favored by Lloyd Stearman. *National Air and Space Museum*

ABOVE: Walter Beech (in front cockpit) with Brice Goldsborough, CEO of the Pioneer Instrument Company, in the J-4 Wright Whirlwind-powered Travel Air in which they won the 1926 Ford Reliability Tour. The airplane was a showcase for Pioneer's aircraft instruments. *National Air and Space Museum*

Lloyd Stearman in Travel Air days, circa 1925. He soon left to design and build his own aircraft. Ironically, he had nothing to do with the airplane to which his name is most linked, the military training biplane of World War II. It was built after he sold Stearman to Boeing and left the company. *National Air and Space Museum*

The Waco 10 was Waco's most popular open-cockpit biplane. Its main difference from the 1925 Waco 9, the company's first airplane that sold in large numbers, was its new airfoil and a fully cowled OX-5 engine. Clayt Bruckner and Sam Yunkin of Waco struggled for years on a shoestring to become successful airplane builders. They were supported in the early years by Buck Weaver, who gave Waco its name.

The Waco 9 was the Weaver Aircraft Company's first truly successful airplane, capable of holding its own against the Travel Air, its chief competitor. Like the Travel Air Model A, it had a steel tube fuselage and was powered by an OX-5 engine. The Waco 9's engine was not as completely cowled (here the cowling is off) and was slightly less expensive. *National Air and Space Museum*

old friend Matty Laird offered him a position as demonstration pilot with the Laird Airplane Company in Wichita, he couldn't refuse. Weaver took up his new position in April 1921, and the *Cootie 2* never flew. Bruckner and Yunkin, who were both pilots by now, began to develop a better understanding of the market. They decided to forget about flivver planes and design a three-place replacement for the Jenny to compete with the Swallow, but with a perennial capital shortage it would be a long haul.

In the meantime, the Laird Airplane Company was slowly turning out a steady trickle of Swallows, but friction was growing between Jake Moellendick and Matty Laird. Laird was president, but since Moellendick provided the capital he felt he didn't always have to consult Laird on important decisions. One decision he made without consulting Laird in the summer of 1921, soon after Buck Weaver came on board, was hiring another demonstration pilot. His name was Walter Beech.

Sergeant Beech had gone to flight school at Rich Field after the war and learned to fly in the venerable Jenny. Then, like countless other pilots with a set of Army wings, he hit the barnstorming trail. He worked with a partner out of Arkansas City, Kansas, but a fierce hangar fire torched his airplane and six others, quickly putting an end to his promising venture. When Moellendick offered him a job, he jumped at it.

Although Beech came to the Laird Airplane Company with only about 250 hours of flying time, which was relatively limited experience compared to what pilots like Weaver had, he was a good pilot with tremendous drive and a quiet determination to make the most of his opportunity. He had a knack for air racing, which was not only the main means of advertising airplanes but, for the winners, also a source of important revenue to subsidize aircraft production. Through the rest of the year Beech was steadily finishing "in the money" at the regional meets and was building valuable experience.

The personality clash between Moellendick and Laird worsened. Its first casualty was Weaver who decided he'd had it with Moellendick's management style. In early 1922 he headed back to Lorain on the strength of rumors that Yunkin and Bruckner were coming up with a real airplane called the Waco 4.

By the fall Laird himself had had it. He was on his way back to Chicago, taking two Swallows and $1,500 with him as compensation for his contributions to the company he was leaving behind. The rift at the top proved to be a break of a different sort for

those in the ranks. In January 1924, Jake Moellendick promoted Walter Beech to general manager and head of sales and made Lloyd Stearman chief engineer. He also renamed the company Swallow Airplane Manufacturing Company and took the reins himself.

While the extra seat was selling the Swallow, sales weren't spectacular. Moellendick and Beech reasoned that the airplane needed to be differentiated to a greater extent from the Jenny to sell better. Therefore, Stearman's first task as chief engineer was to update the Swallow. The project turned into an airplane that superficially continued to resemble the Jenny and was still made of wood and fabric, but was a totally new design.

The wings had a new Clark Y airfoil (which was to become popular on light aircraft in coming years). They were single bay, eliminating the need for the second set of struts on each side. The OX-5 engine was completely covered by a beautiful metal cowl. The engine mounts were on the firewall to allow for the quick re-engining of the airplane with different engine models. The landing gear had a divided axle. The airplane looked much more elegant and sleek than the old Jenny. Its clean crisp lines hinted at Stearman's experience with architectural engineering.

Stearman's new airplane was named the New Swallow. It sold better than its predecessor not only because of the improvements, but also because the old surplus workhorses were finally beginning to give up the ghost and replacement aircraft were needed. One New Swallow customer was Clyde Cessna of Rago,

Kansas. Cessna's farm and contract threshing business was thriving, but he hadn't lost touch with aviation. He continued to tinker with his airplanes on occasion and took to the Swallow with great enthusiasm, giving his nephews, Dwane and Dwight Wallace, their first airplane rides in it.

Lloyd Stearman was an admirer of Anthony Fokker's metal construction techniques, especially his use of steel tubing for fuselage components as early as 1911. Stearman also particularly liked the Fokker D-VII World War I fighter. Fokker's work convinced Stearman that the wooden fuselage was passé. One made of fabric-covered steel tube would be lighter and far stronger. Walter Beech agreed and the two set about on their own time from their own resources to design a steel tube fuselage for the New Swallow.

Beech and Stearman unveiled their creation for Moellendick on a dreary December day in 1924. As Stearman later recalled, the reaction they got wasn't what they had expected. First a string of wildcatter's obscenities, then a dressing down about trying to change the tried-and-true ways. Attempts to reason with Moellendick angered him even more, driving him to taunt his two top executives to quit if they didn't like wood. Beech and Stearman called his bluff and out the door they went. Within months they'd have an airplane manufacturing company of their own.

Stearman and Beech knew exactly what airplane they wanted to build; but again, there was the matter of capital, or rather, the lack of it. The pair succeeded

The Berryloid paint company's advertisement for the Alexander Eaglerock was one in a series of colorful advertisements suitable for framing. The series had a bird theme, depicting an aircraft paint scheme derived from the plumage of particularly colorful species. It illustrates the intense competition among suppliers of the rapidly developing aircraft industry.

HEASUP

This Eaglerock is appropriately finished in Berry Havana Brown, black, white and Waco Maize, after the markings of the Bald Eagle.

EAGLEROCK *with*

Berryloid

AIRCRAFT FINISHES

Bald EAGLE

©1929

Performance Comparison, Early Biplanes

During the first half of the 1920s advances in nontransport aircraft performance were incremental, largely because of the limitations of the OX-5 engine the airplanes shared. The understanding of aerodynamics and construction techniques were evolving slowly, but to get the most out of the OX-5 these early open-cockpit biplanes inevitably had a similar appearance. Significant progress would come only after more capable alternatives to the OX-5 appeared.

	Curtiss	New Swallow	Travel Air	Waco
	JN-4D		Model A -	9
	1917	1924	1925	1925
Engine	OX-5, 90 hp	OX-5, 90 hp	OX-5, 90 hp	OX-5, 90 hp
Seats	2	3	3	3
Max. speed (mph)	75	100	100	92
Cruise speed (mph)	65	85	85	79
Range (stat. miles)	160	450	425	375
Gross weight (lb)	1,920	2,200	2,180	2,100
Useful load (lb)	490	753	845	780
Price	$3,500	$2,750	$3,100	$2,500
	(1924 surplus $500)			

in convincing Harold Innes, a local businessman who was interested in the venture's potential to attract airmail contracts, to provide most of the initial seed capital. More significantly, they persuaded Clyde Cessna to return to aviation and join them as a partner. They named their new company Travel Air Inc.

Initially Cessna invested an amount equal to what Beech could contribute from his air racing winnings. But within a year, when he was more confident of Travel Air's success, Cessna put $25,000 into the company. This was the lion's share of its funding, and he became Travel Air's president.

Travel Air's first airplane gave free expression to Lloyd Stearman's talents and the influence of Anthony Fokker on the young chief engineer's work. Most novel was the light, sturdy steel tube and fabric fuselage, which was given the desired aerodynamic shape with the help of nonstructural wooden former strips.

The wings were single bay structures, like the New Swallow's, and their N struts and fewer support wires gave them a cleaner appearance. Pushrods instead of cables controlled the ailerons, which were on the upper wing only. The airplane was designed to be flyable with one aileron in case of an emergency, and at Beech's insistence it had dual cables running to the elevators for redundancy.

The control surfaces were the most visible evidence of Fokker's influence on Stearman. The rudder and ailerons both had prominent round overhanging tips that aerodynamically balanced the control forces. Their appearance gave the airplane the nickname "Old Elephant Ears."

The venerable OX-5, which was still just about the only viable light aircraft engine available, was fully faired in by a metal cowling, similar to the one Stearman had designed for the New Swallow. The engine mount was bolted to the firewall and could be quickly exchanged for another one to facilitate equipping the airplane with different engines without the need for any airframe alterations. The front cockpit had ample room for two passengers side by side, while in the rear cockpit the pilot sat alone.

The prototype Travel Air was built without the benefit of plans or jigs. Chalk lines drawn on the floor provided guidance for putting the airframe together. There was a tremendous push to get the first airplane completed. The fuselage was being painted on a Sunday to have it mated to the silver doped wings on Monday. Blue was the chosen fuselage color, but the painters discovered that while they had several cans of blue, they didn't have enough in any one can for the

Aviation was an exotic industry in its early years, but the basic materials technology used to build aircraft was well understood. Metal and woodworking techniques applied to making airplanes were not particularly cutting edge. Note the careful safety wiring of the bolts on this propeller attachment. The safety wires are deliberately set in a pattern between bolt pairs to restrain the bolts from unscrewing.

FAR RIGHT: OX-5-powered Command Aire. Although introduced in the late 1920s, like most open-cockpit biplanes of its time, it is representative of the earlier Jenny era. Designed by Albert Voellmecke who had worked for Heinkel in Germany, and built in Little Rock, Arkansas, it was a remarkably stable aircraft. Factory test pilot Ike Vermilya was famous for climbing out of the Command Aire in flight (while flying solo), straddling its fuselage as if he were riding a horse and steering by leaning left and right. *Jim Koepnick/EAA*

whole job. With all the stores closed, in a fit of inspiration they mixed up all the cans into one big vat. And so Travel Air Blue was born, which became the airplane's signature color.

The first Travel Air made a flawless maiden flight in March 1925, and Beech was soon off to the races with it to earn prize money to subsidize the company and drum up sales. The Travel Air was well received, being an improvement over the New Swallow that had won itself much praise for representing the first significant step beyond the Jenny. It added considerable credibility to the reputation of the Travel Air that it was designed by the creator of the New Swallow. Walter Beech promoted the Travel Air's alleged superiority by coining one of his many famous marketing slogans, calling the steel tube cage of the fuselage "the passenger's life preserver."

The Travel Air proved to be a strong seller in spite of its steep $3,500 sticker price. By the middle of 1925 Travel Air Inc. had 15 firm orders. In addition to more workers, the company also desperately needed an office manager. Clyde Cessna hired a sharp and energetic young woman named Olive Ann Mellor for the post. It was the best personnel decision of Cessna's life as far as Walter Beech was concerned. When Beech and Mellor were married five years later they each got not only a spouse but also a business partner for life. And eventually Mrs. Olive Ann Beech would run Beechcraft for over three decades, becoming one of the most highly respected aircraft industry executives of the twentieth century.

While the foundations of a light aircraft industry were being established in Wichita, Kansas, Clayt Bruckner and Sam Yunkin struggled on at Waco in Lorain, Ohio. Perpetually short of funds, they were doggedly making progress with the Waco 4. It essentially had a Jenny fuselage, with the obligatory widening to accommodate two passengers side by side. But its interesting feature, one from which Yunkin and Bruckner were gaining valuable experience, was a new wing based on a new, efficient airfoil, the USA 27. The Waco 4 first took to the air in late 1921 and flew better than a Jenny. It was Waco's first successful airplane, and brought Weaver back into the fold.

There still was, however, the nagging problem of money. The lack of capital prevented Waco from even beginning to make inroads into the strong lead the

The Travel Air factory on East Central, in Wichita, where Raytheon Aircraft (successor to Beechcraft) is still located: This building remains standing, though it is now only a small part of the total Raytheon facility. *National Air and Space Museum*

Standard, which later became Hamilton-Standard, was an early manufacturer of metal propellers for high-performance aircraft. Wood propellers were easy to make and were light but could not be made to enable the blade angles to be adjustable. The development of adjustable pitch for optimizing the blade angle for climb and cruise requirements was a major advance in propeller technology.

Swallow organization had built itself in the tiny market of the day.

To ease the cash crunch and speed up the building of their next aircraft, the Waco trio had an imaginative idea. Why bother building fuselages since the wings were the real story? Why not just convert Jenny fuselages and re-equip them with new wings? That's just what they did with the next four aircraft they built, calling the conversion the Waco 5. At about this time they also moved to Medina, Ohio, into larger premises.

The Waco 5 conversions generated only modest income. Bruckner tried to raise money from his flying friends dating back to the Cicero Field days. As much as they would have liked to invest in Waco, money was tight and Weaver had to face reality once again. For all practical purposes the Weaver Aircraft Company was bankrupt. It may as well be put out of its misery. Bruckner and Yunkin, tenacious as ever and with no mouths to feed but their own, wanted to hang on, hoping against hope for an investor. In early 1923 the Weaver Aircraft Company was dissolved, and its assets transferred to the Advanced Aircraft Company owned by Bruckner and Yunkin. By then Weaver had wished them well and had gone to Chicago to work as an instructor and occasional charter pilot.

Although they stuck with their dream, Bruckner and Yunkin were at their wit's end, but just as they began to seriously entertain the depressing thought of giving it all up, their luck changed. Into their life walked Alden Sampson II, a wealthy ne'er-do-well bon vivant with a fascination for fast cars and airplanes—and a sizable trust fund about to kick in. Sampson had been spending most of his time driving his family to distraction by refusing to take life seriously, but he had a genuine interest in machinery of every sort and immediately hit it off with Bruckner and Yunkin. Within a few weeks a rescue plan was hatched for the Advanced Airplane Company. They were going to get Sampson's family to invest in it in exchange for teaching Sampson the aircraft manufacturing business, which would "make a man out of him."

Clayt and Alden drove to Springfield, Massachusetts, to Sampson's family estate, and the deal was struck. Success was in large measure due to Bruckner's developing natural talent for being a hard-nosed, disciplined businessman and meticulous accountant. The convincing presentation he made put the Advanced Airplane Company back in business—if Sampson didn't kill them both racing his Willis Knight Phaeton back to Ohio.

The funding they received wasn't exorbitant. It was an initial payment for the company's goodwill that would see them through a year or so, with the possibility of more funding later. But that's all Bruckner and Yunkin needed.

They moved the Advanced Aircraft Company to Troy, Ohio, to be as close as possible to the aeronautical research activity going on at McCook Field in nearby Dayton. They then set to work building their next airplane. It was the Waco 6. The pair had decided to continue calling their aircraft the Waco as a tribute to all that Weaver had done for them to get them started.

The Waco 6 had a redesigned wing with rounded wing tips and a steel tube empennage. It was lighter than the Waco 4 and flew about as well as a Swallow. It first flew in the summer of 1923, and by the end of the year four of them had been sold. Things were looking up.

In 1924 the Waco 6 got an improved version of its original airfoil and became the Waco 7. The change added 5 miles per hour to cruise speed, a significant improvement in its day. As visitors to McCook Field took note of the small company making biplanes nearby, enough word spread in the market about them to sell 12 Waco 7s in 1924. It was a major accomplishment, but it was immediately threatened by the appearance of Lloyd Stearman's sleeker, faster New Swallow. There was another dark moment in this first really successful year that Bruckner and Yunkin had had in a long time. Buck Weaver, their friend and erstwhile mentor, survivor of all those hours of barnstorming and test flying, died from blood poisoning.

As Buck Weaver would have wanted them to, Bruckner and Yunkin moved swiftly to counter the threat from the New Swallow. In April 1925 they brought out the Waco 9. It was the winner they had dreamed of for years, the airplane that firmly established Waco as a player in aviation. It looked much like a Travel Air without elephant ears, and like the Travel Air, it had a steel tube fuselage. (Bruckner had been teaching himself to weld for some time.) Its OX-5 engine was faired in, but not entirely, unlike the Travel Air and New Swallow.

The similarities in construction to the Travel Air are interesting because the two aircraft were developed concurrently, making it difficult for one manufacturer to "copy" the other. This is another example of the quest for perfection in aviation generally yielding similar results with similar technology.

The Waco 9 was a strong seller from the outset. It would find 47 customers by year's end compared to 19 Travel Airs, which cost about $1,000 more, and against which it had only about a three-month head start. And the next year the company would be making 15 Waco 9s a *month*. The Waco had arrived.

A beautifully laminated propeller made by the Sensenich brothers. For light aircraft powered by engines under 150 horsepower, the fixed pitch wood propeller remained a staple until the 1950s. Even today it is used in specialty applications such as aerobatics where its greater flexibility is more suited to absorbing high acceleration rates than metal propellers, thereby providing more protection to the engine's crankshaft.

The Travel Air came out only in the summer of 1925, but the company lost no time in its efforts to make a big splash with the public. Beech had been long convinced that few accomplishments translate into sales as effectively as victories at air races. He also understood that springing something on the crowds that is extraordinary but not too far removed from the company's product line has great publicity value. With the Tulsa, Oklahoma, Air Races fast approaching, Travel Air maximized its opportunity for publicity by developing and entering an exceptionally fast aircraft. Called the Special, it resembled the original Travel Air but had superior performance.

Stearman had three months to get the Special from concept to the start line and he made it, but only barely. The Special's very first flight was the 90-minute hop to the Tulsa Air Races. It was constructed along the lines of the Travel Air and there were many commonalties, but it was basically a different airplane. The elephant ears were gone, the fuselage was shorter and lighter, and the rudder was a rakish, smooth extension of the fuselage. Up front was a 160-horsepower Curtiss inline C6A engine instead of the anemic OX-5, and the cooling radiator could be raised

The Fairchild F-71 was a development of the FC-2. The FC-2 was designed by Fairchild in 1925 because he couldn't find an airplane on the market to serve as a suitable camera platform for his aerial mapping business. Basic requirements were an enclosed and heated cabin with generous space for bulky camera equipment and a stable camera platform. The design and its derivatives proved so successful that Fairchild found a ready market as a utility airplane and also saw corporate use.
Richard Vander Meulen

into the fuselage to minimize drag when the engine was running sufficiently cool. And if that wasn't enough to get attention, the Special had a glittering gold wing and a jet-black fuselage.

Cruising at 120 to 125 miles per hour, the Special was so fast relative to the competition that Walter Beech could ham it up by deliberately starting dead last and overtaking the whole field to win. The company's stock airplanes also did well, doing better than the Swallows and the Waco 9. For Waco just being present and making a credible effort was reward enough, and its lower prices drew their share of customers for the moment. And Yunkin and Bruckner were already thinking about the next model.

An important development in 1925 was the announcement of the Ford Reliability Tour, which became a major benchmark of aircraft performance. The Aviation Board of the Detroit Board of Commerce came up with the idea of a tour to promote the safety and reliability of aviation, similar to the automobile tours organized a generation before. Entrants would fly a prescribed course of 2,000 miles and would have to come as close as they could to maintaining an average speed of 80 miles per hour. Points would be deducted for lower performance, but each airplane was to race only against its airspeed indicator. The Fords were already in the process of getting into the

This is a good illustration of the steel-tube fuselage frame structure that became the standard construction technique in the mid-1920s. This airplane is the prototype Travel Air. Note the wide front seat with room for two passengers. The engine is the venerable OX-5. *National Air and Space Museum*

The Fairchild FC-2, custom designed in 1925 to serve as a camera platform for Fairchild's aerial mapping cameras, after Fairchild couldn't find a suitable production airplane. *National Air and Space Museum*

air transport business that would lead to the famous Ford Trimotor, so Edsel Ford decided to donate $50,000 and a giant gold-and-silver trophy to the event; hence the name, Ford Reliability Tour.

The chief instigator of the tour on the board of commerce was William A. Mara, and for help in making the aeronautical arrangements he relied on his good friend Eddie Stinson. Since the end of World War I, Eddie had been a barnstormer, test pilot, and the personal pilot of a Mexican general, among other adventures. He and a friend had flown a four-passenger Junkers low-wing monoplane 26 hours and 19 minutes over Long Island nonstop to break the world endurance record.

The all-metal German Junkers was a remarkably advanced small airliner for its time. Its passenger cabin was enclosed, the pilot, and if desired, a copilot (who was usually the mechanic) sat up front in the nose, and it had a cantilevered wing. In the summer of 1922 Stinson established the Stinson Flying Service with a Junkers based out of Detroit to benefit from the business of the rich automobile industry executives. His corrugated metal machine became a fixture on the Detroit-Chicago route, and he flew the first nonstop commercial night flight between Chicago and New York with a wealthy feed merchant for a passenger.

When the Ford Reliability Tour was being organized, Stinson and Mara surveyed and set out the course in the Junkers. The week-long tour was a great success. Flown in the fall, it drew 17 participants, including Swallows, Travel Airs, and Wacos and was seen in those days before television by hundreds of thousands of spectators. Three Travel Airs, to Walter Beech's great satisfaction, and one Swallow received perfect scores. The tour also encouraged Eddie Stinson to act on the plan he had been formulating for some time to build a four-seat, enclosed-cabin biplane.

Stinson turned to Mara for assistance in securing the all-important capital to build his airplane. Mara relied on his board of commerce connections to put together an investor's syndicate, and a well-capitalized Stinson was on his way. He was a much better businessman than his barnstormer's flamboyance suggested, and he hired three professionals to help: his longtime mechanic, a talented young engineer named William Naylor, and a University of Detroit consultant in aerodynamics.

By January 1926 the Stinson SB-1 Detroiter was ready (B stood for biplane). In addition to the enclosed cabin that included the pilot's seat, other features radical for the time were an electric starter and brakes. Its construction was the typical steel tube wood and fabric of the day, but its engine was special.

The Detroiter was one of the first airplanes to be equipped with the new, efficient, lightweight 200-horsepower Wright J-4 Whirlwind radial engine. The Whirlwind represented a landmark development in engine technology that would allow light aircraft to break away from the limitations of the tired old OX-5.

The first flight of the Stinson Detroiter was on January 26 with Eddie Stinson at the controls. It was perfect in spite of the freezing winter day. In February Stinson invited the public to a demonstration and hopped some 80 passengers. A month later, Horace Dodge, the automobile mogul, paid Stinson $12,500 for the Detroiter.

In short order a second Detroiter was sold to Dodge's cousin. This track record was enough to prompt turning the investment syndicate into the Stinson Aircraft Corporation in May 1926, and to convince Bill Mara to leave the board of commerce to join Eddie Stinson full time. Personal and corporate aviation's era of the large cabin-class airplane had begun.

The story of personal and corporate aviation between 1919 and 1926 is largely the story of the Jennies, Swallows, Travel Airs, and Wacos. But by the mid-1920s, as interest in aviation continued to grow, there were

The Stinson SB-1 Detroiter. Eddie Stinson's first entry into the aircraft manufacturing business and the cabin class. Based on his air charter business, Stinson was convinced that the future lay in the cabin airplane. The SB-1 was one of the first airplanes to be powered by a Wright Whirlwind engine and also featured brakes and a starter, both relative novelties at the time.

The Stinson SM-1 in an early corporate role serving the Packard Corporation. The SM-1 was the first of the classic Detroiter monoplane line. Stinson abandoned the biplane configuration after the SB-1 in favor of the more efficient monoplane design. *National Air and Space Museum*

numerous other initiatives, several of which would grow in significance. Since building aircraft was essentially a custom craft and the choices were limited, it wasn't unusual for business people in need of an airplane to form an enterprise to design one from scratch rather than go to an established manufacturer. Three good examples of this approach during the mid-1920s, which led to the founding of aircraft makers that would make a difference, are the Alexander Eaglerock, the first Fairchild, and the Ryan M.

All J. Don Alexander knew of airplanes in 1924 was the rumor that they were becoming an efficient way of getting around. He spent most of his days surrounded by attractive, often scantily clad young women. J. Don was the president of the Alexander Film Company of Englewood, Colorado, premiere producer of the commercials that bombarded movie-goers before there was television.

With all the publicity that airplanes were getting, it occurred to J. Don that an airborne sales force could

Eddie Stinson (center) with the Junkers monoplane he operated in the early 1920s. His experience with the Junkers convinced him that the enclosed cabin airplane was the way to go in personal/corporate aviation. *National Air and Space Museum*

Working on their cranky engines in the field was an everyday event for the pilots of the 1920s. They had to be mechanics as much as they were pilots. It wasn't uncommon to experience a problem in-flight, land in the first suitable field, fix the engine, and take off again.

By the mid-1920s most aircraft had a rudimentary altimeter. Diaphragm barometers were common by then, and the concept was easily adaptable to altimeters. Accuracy, however, was another matter. On record altitude flights, altimeters and the sealed barographs used for registering the record could be off from each other by as much as several thousand feet.

greatly increase lingerie commercial sales. His top salesman soon was taking flying lessons from Benny Howard in a used company Swallow, and when J. Don realized that no manufacturer was in a position to deliver 50 to 60 airplanes to his film studio at once, he decided to go into the airplane-making business.

The task of designing the Alexander Airplane Company's first airplane fell on Dan Noonan, who lately had been engaged in designing new wings for Jennies being modified by Nicholas-Beazley. The effort came up with the catchy name of Eaglerock for the airplane, but otherwise the creation of the prototype, which resembled a fat New Swallow, wasn't a happy experience. It would barely fly at Englewood's 6,000 feet altitude with one on board, and when J. Don came out to be taken for his first ride all that ensued was a lot of furious taxiing about.

To fix the problem J. Don turned to a 19-year-old high school graduate and avid modeler named Al Mooney. Mooney's nonexistent engineering experience wasn't questioned. He was asked only whether or not he could make the Eaglerock fly. When he answered in the affirmative, he was given the chance.

Mooney designed a whole new Eaglerock that resembled the Travel Air complete with the Fokker D-VII–style rudder and the obligatory OX-5 engine. Not only did it look like a Travel Air, but it also flew like one, and the Alexander Airplane Company was in business. It would go on to make more than 900 Eaglerocks in the next four years—but its sales force never learned to fly.

Sherman Fairchild had more of an interest than J. Don Alexander in aviation. He was an inventor and maker of aerial mapping cameras and founder and operator of Fairchild Aerial Surveys based on Long Island, New York. He needed a suitable airplane to run his business but couldn't find one. Doing aerial mapping from high altitude required a large enclosed and heated cabin, and a high-wing monoplane to give the downward looking cameras the maximum view possible. Fairchild decided his only solution was to build the airplane himself and gave his own engineering department the task.

The conventionally constructed FC-1 first flew in June 1926 with an OX-5 engine. Though underpowered, it performed acceptably, even reaching 9,800 feet on subsequent test flights. It was a rock-solid camera platform. A second prototype, equipped with the

new 200-horsepower J-4 Whirlwind radial engine, was perfect. Fairchild had his camera plane, but he soon realized that he also had an airplane for which there was a market and the Fairchild Aircraft Company would become a highly respected airplane maker.

T. Claude Ryan also got into aircraft manufacturing because he was interested in a purpose-built airplane that was unavailable. Until 1925 the U.S. Army had car-

ried all the airmail following a disastrous experience with early civilian experiments. But that was changing, and Ryan, a San Diego, California–based operator of Ryan Airlines, wanted an airplane that could haul more mail for less expense than the airplanes available.

Ryan decided on a high-wing monoplane design, which he felt was more efficient than the biplanes in terms of load bearing and had a big cargo space. The airplane had an open cockpit, but the one-piece wing was mounted too close to the top of the fuselage. Ryan had in-house talent to do the job. His staff had done a lot of modification work on the company's Standards and the first Douglas, a big 12-passenger biplane that Ryan Airlines used on its daily runs to Los Angeles.

The conventionally constructed monoplane that Ryan, his partner, Franklin Mahoney, and their shop superintendent, Hawley Bowlus, came up with was the M-1. It flew well with its 150-horsepower inline Hisso engine, but Ryan recognized it could benefit from a lighter, less complicated wing. His friend Donald Douglas

recommended a young aeronautical engineer named John Northrop for the job. With the new wing, the Ryan, now renamed the M-2, was popular enough to find 18 customers (nine M-1's were built) and make Ryan an aircraft manufacturer of some recognition. It was a small step to enclose the M-2's cabin, develop the Brougham line, and fill a special order called the *Spirit of St. Louis*.

By 1926 making personal and business airplanes was becoming big business. The yearly output of the top manufacturers no longer numbered in the dozens but in the hundreds. Demand was strong enough to prompt an increasing number of entrepreneurs to get into aircraft design and manufacturing. As aerial activity and airplane construction mushroomed, a perceived need for oversight was growing stronger, and big changes were on the way. The government was about to impose strict standards and much greater supervision over every aspect of aviation. And on his lonely mail runs in the ink-black night, a lanky farm boy from Minnesota was planning a flight that would drive America plane crazy.

ABOVE INSET: Airspeed indicator, circa 1920. It is mounted to the wing strut, visible to the pilot, with the spring-loaded tab facing the direction of flight. The tab is pushed back by the airflow, indicating the correct airspeed. Note the red area on the dial indicating stall range.

This 180-horsepower Hisso (Hispano Suiza) powered Travel Air is in the exact configuration and color scheme as it was when it was flown in the 1926 Ford Reliability Tour by Clarence Clark. The current owner barnstormed with the airplane in the 1930s and sold it. In 1978 he bought it back and has been flying it on the antique circuit ever since. Because of the Hisso's shape, this airplane looks quite similar to the original OX-5-powered Travel Air.

CHAPTER 3

AIR AGE

Nineteen twenty-six was a watershed year for American aviation. In recognition of the increasing complexity of designing, building, and operating aircraft, and the growing potential risk to the general public, the U.S. Congress passed the Air Commerce Act of 1926. It was sweeping legislation that made it the government's responsibility to set standards for the aviation industry to safeguard the public interest.

A licensing system was introduced for pilots and mechanics. Standards were established for the design and construction of aircraft. Before an airplane or an aero engine could be offered for sale, it would have to pass rigorous evaluation by the Aviation Division of the Department of Commerce and be issued an Approved Type Certificate (ATC). A lesser, so-called Group 2 approval was also instituted for very small production runs or the minor modification of an existing design.

The ATC requirement was to take effect in 1927. In addition to new designs, it was to apply retroactively to all aircraft that were designed before the passage of the legislation and were still in production.

Another landmark development that began to make itself felt with full force in the personal aircraft industry during 1926 was the breakthrough in engine design that would free light aircraft from the limitations of the OX-5 and similar liquid-cooled inline engines. The harbinger of change was the air-cooled 200-horsepower J-4 Wright Whirlwind radial engine, introduced, as mentioned earlier, during the previous year. While it weighed approximately the same as the OX-5, it could put out more than twice the power. This doubled its power-to-weight ratio to 0.40 horsepower per pound compared to the OX-5's 0.20 horsepower per pound. (Subsequent Whirlwind models were even lighter and put out more power.)

The J-4 was Wright's commercialization of an engine developed by Charles L. Lawrence with backing from the U.S. Navy. In 1926 the J-4 was superseded by the improved 220-horsepower J-5 Whirlwind, which gained a reputation for being one of the most reliable aircraft engines of its day. It got Lindbergh to Paris and secured the 1927 Collier Trophy for Lawrence.

Competing engine makers rushed to play catch-up to the Wright J-4 and -5, for which demand quickly outraced supply. Curtiss and Lycoming offered competing models, and Warner and Kinner developed the less powerful, lighter radials for the smaller airframes.

By the second half of the 1920s aircraft makers could choose from several air-cooled radials with improved power-to-weight ratios, power output ranging between 90 and 450 horsepower, and greater service reliability. Widening the envelope in engine performance greatly increased the capabilities of the

The Waco CSO on floats. As indicated by the Waco code, the engine is a Wright Whirlwind (C), the wings are straight (S), and the fuselage is a type 10 (O). The coding Waco adopted after the Waco 10 looked more confusing than it was. Many of the airplanes of the 1920s and 1930s were on floats. Airports were few and far between, and the nations' many waterways and lakes provided natural airfields. Floats were expensive, however, adding as much as a third to an airplane's price, and there was a substantial speed penalty. *Jim Koepnick/EAA*

A gorgeous Taperwing Waco CTO restored by Ted Davis. The Taperwing Waco, introduced in 1928, gave Waco the panache it had lacked before. Flying a Taperwing Waco, Johnny Livingston won the 1928 National Air Race from New York to Los Angeles, beating Charles "Speed" Hollman in a Laird Solution. The Taperwing became best known for its excellent aerobatic performance. The tapered wings are interchangeable with the straight wings, characteristic of the flexible, frugal design mentality at Waco.

three-seat open-cockpit biplane and also made viable the cabin-class personal airplane.

These advances coincided with an increasingly vibrant economy as the Roaring Twenties built up steam. The demand for personal and business aircraft was up sharply by 1926, allowing companies like Waco and Travel Air to progress from focusing intensively on developing aircraft to producing them in high volumes. The Department of Commerce's ATC tests validated the soundness of the wood, fabric, and steel tube construction formula, which would change little for more than two decades.

Thus it was already an optimistic time for the aircraft industry by the summer of 1927 when Charles Lindbergh coaxed the *Spirit of St. Louis* into the air from New York's Roosevelt Field one foggy morning. His

33 1/2-hour flight to Paris won him the $25,000 Orteig Prize for being the first to fly nonstop between the two cities and whipped the American public's interest in aviation into an unprecedented frenzy. The already increasing demand for the airplanes of the established manufacturers soared, and a parade of new entrants flooded the market, eager to cash in on the decade's hottest industry.

Travel Air was in a strong position by the time the Wright J-4 engine became available and the Air Commerce Act was passed. The first J-4-powered Travel Air was sold in January 1926. Over the next few years the company's main efforts with the maturing Travel Air line were concentrated on making it available with a wider variety of engines to broaden the product line.

The OX-5-powered model continued to be offered as an entry level airplane for the remainder of the decade and became the Travel Air 2000. A 150-horsepower Hisso-powered version became the Travel Air 3000, and the Wright J-4-powered version became the Travel Air 4000. As the J-4 gave way to the J-5 and other brands of air-cooled radials appeared, they were also mated to the Model 4000 airframe and designated Model 4000 variants.

The reason airplanes of all manufacturers powered by the OX-5 (and its 100-horsepower derivative, the OXX-6) continued to be in popular demand was price. The surplus OX-5 could still be had for as little as $250, while the new J-4 Whirlwind engine cost $5,000, considerably more than an entire OX-5-powered Travel Air, Waco, or Eaglerock.

It was possible to install a wide range of different engines with minor changes to the Travel Air's airframe because, as the DOT certification tests were to prove, Lloyd Stearman had built a healthy safety margin into his design. From a structural integrity standpoint the only changes required for handling the performance increases provided by the higher powered engines was the use of higher gauge material in some of the metal components and slightly thicker spars.

A great achievement for Travel Air in 1926 was the performance of a Travel Air equipped with a Wright J-4 engine in the Ford Reliability Tour of that year. The rules had changed since the first tour. A winner was declared, and that winner was the Travel Air flown by Walter Beech himself.

The airplane was a production model cosponsored in the tour by Pioneer Instrument Company to

A fine portrait of a Laird Commercial introduced in the late 1920s. In the hands of Charles "Speed" Hollman and E. E. Ballaugh, Laird Commercials took first and second place in the 1927 Spokane-to-Washington National Air Races. They were expensive custom-built aircraft for the sports pilot. *National Air and Space Museum*

Matty Laird's personal 1928 Laird Commercial (restored by Ken Love) meets 1931 Waco QCF on short final. Laird flew this Commercial throughout the 1930s and even took his honeymoon in it in 1933. In 1982 he flew it again with his wife shortly before he passed away.

The Wright Whirlwind engine allowed personal aviation to break out of the venerable 90- to 100-horsepower OX-5 constraint. First example was the 200-horsepower Wright J-4. It earned its creator, Charles L. Lawrence, the Collier Trophy after a 220-horsepower J-5 took Lindbergh safely across the Atlantic on his epic flight to Paris.

Following Wright's lead, Lycoming also got into the radial game. This Stinson Detroiter is equipped with a 220-horsepower Lycoming engine. Originally Detroiters had Wrights, but when E. L. Cord, which owned Lycoming, bought Stinson the switch was made.

promote its aviation instruments, particularly its recently invented earth inductor compass. This was the first vacuum-driven heading indicator set by the standard magnetic compass and gave much more stable display of heading especially during turns (vacuum pressure was provided by a venturi mounted on the fuselage). The earth inductor compass was a major development in aerial navigation, which would be one of the most valued instruments on board the *Spirit of St. Louis* and other record-breaking aircraft in coming years. Navigating for Beech on the Ford Reliability Tour was Pioneer's CEO, Brice Goldsborough.

Walter Beech continued to push for the publicity to be had from racing and record flying. In 1927 he introduced a young woman named Louise Thaden to flying. Within two years she set a women's altitude record of 20,200 feet in a Travel Air 3000 and won the first transcontinental Women's Air Derby in a Travel Air 4000.

As demand for the Travel Air biplane began approaching the company's production capacity, Clyde Cessna revived an old obsession of his, the monoplane. Fully occupied with the challenges of

increasing production, Beech and the company's other directors weren't inclined to divert scarce resources to experimenting with a monoplane, but saw no reason to object to the company's president working on one on his own time.

The airplane Clyde Cessna designed and built during his off-hours in 1926 was a high-wing monoplane with a semi-cantilevered wing, powered by a 10-cylinder 110-horsepower air-cooled Anzani. It was capable of hoisting 1,000 pounds aloft, and when Walter Beech flew it he was impressed. The timing of the new monoplane was perfect. In 1925 the government had privatized the carriage of air mail, and a company called National Air Transport (NAT) had obtained the Chicago Dallas route. NAT was looking for a new, more capable airplane than its aging fleet of Curtiss Carrier Pigeons to carry both passengers and the mail and had put out a bid. Cessna's monoplane would be the basis for Travel Air's entry.

The production airplane the company developed from Cessna's monoplane was the Travel Air 5000. Powered by a Wright J-4 and capable of hoisting a

The EAA's replica *Spirit of St. Louis*. Lindbergh canvassed all the manufacturers when he was looking for a suitable airplane for his quest for the $25,000 Oertig Prize for being first to fly between New York and Paris. T. Claude Ryan offered an excellent airplane at the most reasonable price. Ironically he had sold the firm by the time construction began on Lindbergh's airplane. *Jim Koepnick/EAA*

The Ryan M-2 was the predecessor to the *Spirit of St. Louis*, developed by T. Claude Ryan to compete for the mail contracts that were put out for civilian bid in 1925 after being flown by the military. The engine is an inline 150-horsepower Hispano Suiza (Hisso). Eighteen M-2s were built. *National Air and Space Museum*

Mystery Ship

The Travel Air most famous in its time wasn't a biplane or a cabin monoplane off the company's product line but a custom-built racer, the R-100 Mystery Ship. It was originally the idea of Herb Rawdon, a talented young Travel Air engineer who wanted to challenge the Army's dominance of the closed-circuit speed events at the national air races during the 1920s. Rawdon was inspired by the sleek monoplanes that were appearing in one of aviation's most famous speed races, the Schneider Cup, flown exclusively by custom-built seaplanes (the Supermarine winner of the 1931 Schneider Cup was the ancestor of the Spitfire fighter). Rawdon envisioned a Schneider Trophy monoplane without the pontoons.

Working on their own time, Rawdon and his colleague Walter Burnham developed the design that got the old racing spirit fired up in Walter Beech and a green light for the project. To be built in great secrecy, the R-100 would be launched at the 1929 National Air Races in Cleveland. The rumors that started circulating about the hush-hush airplane gave it its popular name, the Mystery Ship.

The Mystery Ship was a low-winged monoplane with wire-braced wings and an airframe covered entirely in plywood. After experiments with a 250- to 300-horsepower Chevrolair inline engine that overheated, its standard engine was a 420-horsepower Wright radial, streamlined by a NACA cowl. In its initial speed tests it achieved speeds of up to 225

A rare aerial photo of the TEXACO Mystery Ship.

miles per hour, about 20 miles per hour above expectations. It was ready for the nationals.

The 1929 free-for-all was the first Thompson Trophy race, sponsored by Charles Thompson whose company made automotive and aircraft valves. The Mystery Ship created quite a buzz when it was unveiled before the public. It became a sensation when in the hands of Doug Davis it won the Thompson Trophy with a blistering average speed of 195 miles per hour, beating an Army Curtiss Hawk fighter. Its speed could have been even higher, but Davis missed a pylon and had to circle back to round it.

The Mystery Ship ushered in the era of the custom-built low-wing civilian monoplane in unlimited racing that led to airplanes like the Granville Brothers' Gee Bees, the Weddell Williams 44, and the Laird-Turner LTR-14. Several Mystery Ships were built. Jimmy Doolittle flew one sponsored by Shell Oil. Frank Hawks set more than 200 records in the best-publicized Mystery Ship, the Texaco 13. And Pancho Barnes bought serial number 1 and broke the women's straight-line world speed record in it. When Travel Air was bought by Curtiss Wright, there were plans to put the R-100 in full-scale production, but the Depression shelved these plans.

---

hefty 1,200 pounds of useful load, it fully met NAT's requirements. In January 1927 Travel Air became a manufacturer of cabin monoplanes when it was awarded the contract by NAT to build eight Model 5000s.

Stearman and Cessna had been collaborating on the Travel Air 5000, but before the airplane was completed Lloyd Stearman announced that he was leaving for Venice, California, to establish his own company. He would design and build a biplane based on his experience with the Travel Airs. His place was taken by Horace Weihlmiller, an aeronautical engineer with a degree from the Massachusetts Institute of Technology and experience at the Army's McCook research facility.

Cessna wrapped up the Travel Air 5000 project and then, he too, tendered his resignation. His independent and creative mind was drawing him away from the humdrum business of running a factory to designing yet another monoplane, this one with a fully cantilevered wing.

The Travel Air 5000 soon put the company's name in the headlines. Only days after Lindbergh's flight to Paris, the Dole Pineapple Company announced a $25,000 prize for the first civilian airplane to reach Hawaii from the U.S. mainland. Travel Air 5000s had the distinction of accomplishing this feat not once, but twice. Odd as that may sound, everything is possible when a major American corporation's pineapple sales are at stake.

On July 15, a month and a half after the Dole prize announcement, the prototype Travel Air 5000 made it to Hawaii with owner/pilot Ernest Smith and his navigator, Emory Bronte, on board after flying through the night from Oakland, California. They didn't qualify for the prize, however, because Dole had specified August 12 as the earliest start date, presumably to give time for a sufficient number of entrants to materialize so that the group of participants would be suitably large to properly promote pineapples.

Stearman C-3 in its element. Lloyd Stearman struck out on his own in 1926 shortly after designing the Travel Air Model A. The C-3 was the first of his designs that sold in large numbers. Its lines clearly resembled the one-of-a-kind Travel Air Special Stearman designed for the 1925 racing season to earn Travel Air prize money and publicity. *Jack Greiner/Antique Airplane Association*

By the late 1920s with more than two dozen aviation firms, including aircraft makers and their suppliers, based in Wichita, it was not too much of a stretch to call it the Air Capital. The airplane is a C-3 Stearman. Following a brief stint in cramped quarters in Venice, California, after he left Travel Air in 1926, Stearman soon moved back to Wichita. *National Air and Space Museum*

And so, on August 16, 1927, Art Goebel, the flamboyant and highly skilled stunt pilot and his navigator, William Davis, hauled *Woolaroc*, another Travel Air 5000, into the air from Oakland. They were among six participants winging their way toward Hawaii (two more had tried but crashed on takeoff). More than 26 hours later, *Woolaroc* landed safely at Wheeler Field to pocket Dole's $25,000 for being the first civilian airplane to do the trip, more than a month after another Travel Air 5000 had, in fact, been the first to do so. The Model 5000 would be shortly developed into the Travel Air 6000, which would enjoy some success as a small airliner and corporate airplane.

The Spartan C-3 Wright powered
with the Wright J-6 150 h.p. motor

ABOVE, RIGHT AND OPPOSITE:
The Spartan C-3 was put in
production with the financial clout of
oil man Bill Skelly, whose company
bought the Mid-Continent Aircraft
Company, designers of the airplane,
for a million dollars. The C-3 was the
primary trainer of the Spartan School
of Aeronautics. The airplane pictured
has been flown by the same owner,
Ed Wegner, since 1967.

While it took nothing away from
Goebel's skillful performance, the race turned
into quite a fiasco when only one other airplane made it, three turned back, and one was
never seen again. Profoundly affected by the
event was Jake Moellendick's Swallow
Airplane Manufacturing Company. Their
entry, developed specifically for the race,
was one of the airplanes that had returned
to Oakland. Later it was gallantly volun-
teered to look for the disappeared contes-
tant, and it too was never seen again.

Maintaining leadership in design and in-
flexible standards of workmanship, Spartan
Aircraft Company adds to its line the Spartan
C-3 powered with the Wright J-6. Now a
famous plane and a famous motor provide a
combination which cannot fail in its appeal to
all who recognize and appreciate correct balance between an airplane and its power plant.

The Spartan C-3 Wright is destined to
make new Spartan history on the airways. It
retains all the supreme qualities of Spartan
design — riding comfort, stability, constant
reliability — qualities synonymous with the
name Spartan. To those acquainted with the

Spartan pledge and policy this new plane
needs no recommendation except that it has
been rigorously and scientifically tested and
proclaimed by engineers a credit to its name.

The Spartan is a distinctly superior airplane because in the Spartan organization
there is a spirit of high obligation to the
ultimate owner. Production goes forward
steadily and at a pace that strives for quality
rather than quantity. There has never been
a Spartan structural failure.

SPARTAN AIRCRAFT COMPANY
TULSA ·· OKLAHOMA

A folder describing the new Spartan C-3 Wright will be sent on request.

Swallow, which had gone on making Lloyd Stearman's New Swallow, had recently switched to a welded steel tube fuselage (ironically designed by Lloyd's brother, Waverly), but had no pending new designs. It could have used the benefits of a good showing in the Dole race.

As the freewheeling days of aviation were coming to a close with the imminence of the Air Commerce Act, the Advanced Aircraft Company of Troy, Ohio, was firmly establishing its position as a leading maker of personal airplanes with the Waco 9. While only slightly less capable with its semi-enclosed OX-5 than the similarly engined Travel Air, the Waco 9 was about 30 percent less expensive, which made it a strong seller. Like the Travel Air, it was also available with the OX-5 derivative, the 100 HP OXX-6.

By mid-1926 Clayt Bruckner and Sam Yunkin were building Waco 9s at a rate that soared as high as 15 airplanes per month, but they were also beginning to think of a more capable successor. The two friends had stuck to their goal of becoming successful airplane makers with rare tenacity, but now, with a bright future before them, tragedy struck. Sam Yunkin died from an illness. It was only a little over a year since their mentor, Buck Weaver, had died.

Now Bruckner was alone, and it took all his perseverance to push on. In large measure he was able keep the Advanced Airplane Company going after Yunkin's death because he was joined by Buck Weaver's barnstorming partner, Charlie Meyers, as test pilot and head of design and development.

Meyers' first priority was the development of the Waco 10, which first flew in the spring of 1927 and got its ATC in the fall. Originally equipped with the OX-5 engine, which was now fully cowled, the Waco 10 had a redesigned empennage, a wide base split axle landing gear assembly, and a slightly redesigned wing free of the Model 9's aerodynamically balanced "elephant ear" ailerons.

The Waco 10's performance was competitive and its handling delightful, but its commercial success also had a lot to do with Bruckner's business ability. He had matured into an extremely capable manager, one of the most bottom-line-oriented executives in the industry. He introduced mass production techniques at Waco to the maximum extent possible, which kept production costs firmly in check and enabled the company to price the Waco 10 about 20 percent, or $500, below the competition.

Demand for the new Waco received a big boost when Charlie Meyers flew an OX-5-powered Waco 10 to victory in its class in the 1927 National Air Race from New York to Spokane, Washington. The 10 flew the 2,352-mile dis-

tance in 30 hours and 23 minutes, beating an Alexander Eaglerock by 28 minutes. The company knew it had its biggest winner to date when, by the end of 1927, 360 OX-powered Waco 10s had been sold, making it the best-selling airplane in America.

As the Wright Whirlwind and other air-cooled radial engines became available, the Waco 10 underwent the same diversification as the Travel Air. Its airframe remained basically unchanged through the decade but was available with a number of powerplant options. It is from this time that the Waco alphabet soup model designation originated. The first coded Waco was the ASO, a Waco 10 powered by a 220-horsepower J-5 Wright Whirlwind. Pilots remembered it more readily as the Whirlwind Waco.

The Wacos of the mid-1920s were considered to be among the most reliable aircraft of their type, but they had more of a reputation as sensible rather than racy airplanes. That, however, all changed with the appearance in 1928 of the Taperwing Waco that would go down in history as one of the flashiest biplanes ever.

The Taperwing idea originated with Charlie Meyers who, as an old, red-blooded barnstormer, recognized that the Waco could use a sportier image. He convinced Bruckner to let him try a slick-looking tapered wing that would have a new NACA M-6 airfoil, which would make the airplane faster than the Waco 10 and competitive in cross-country racing, so important to image building.

With characteristic common sense, Bruckner had Meyers design the wing to be interchangeable with the traditional straight wing. The Taperwing Waco first

Skelly Oil Company, owner of the Spartan Aircraft Company and the Spartan School of Aeronautics, derived significant revenue from its aviation gasoline and oil business. It is interesting to note the developed airway structure connecting Oklahoma City, Denver, and St. Louis by the end of the 1920s.

mass of the more uniformly built rectangular wing, thereby reducing rolling inertia and giving it a phenomenal roll rate for its time. Upper and lower ailerons contributed to its agility.

In the hands of famed air show pilot, "Fearless" Freddie Lund, who replaced Charlie Meyers when the latter moved on to new challenges testing the Great Lakes biplanes, the Taperwing Waco became one of the hottest ships on the aerobatic scene. About 60 Taperwing Wacos were made in all. Known at different times as the 10-T, the 220 Sport Taperwing, the ATO, and the CTO (with a 225-horsepower J-6) as the company's designation system changed, the Taperwing Waco remains one of the most seductive open-cockpit biplanes among the antiques.

While Clayt Bruckner and his colleagues were developing the Waco 10, Lloyd Stearman was crafting his first design, the C-1, as master of his own shop. Only one was built, and it looked remarkably like the Travel Air Special that Stearman had built for the 1925 Tulsa Meet. The design was quickly refined into the C-2, initially powered by an OX-5 but intended for the Wright J-4 and other more powerful engines.

Venice proved not to be an ideal location for Stearman. When Walter Innes of Wichita and several business associates invited him back to the "Air Capital of the World" and offered to invest in his business to make it a viable manufacturer, Stearman happily moved back to his old haunt. The C-2 was followed by the C-3, which was essentially identical, except for an engine upgrade to the 220-horsepower Wright J-5.

Stearman chose to concentrate on the high end of the market, offering lower-powered versions of his airplanes on a limited custom basis. He had a good run producing mail planes and attracting well-to-do-pilots in search of a rugged, powerful biplane. He also had some success selling the C-3 as a trainer to armed forces abroad.

Matty Laird took to a greater extreme Stearman's approach of making high-end, finely crafted, open-cockpit, three-place biplanes for a limited clientele. As Travel Air and Waco were practically going into mass production, Laird concentrated on custom building ever since he left Swallow and returned to Chicago. Equipped with Wright Whirlwinds as soon as they became available, his black-and-gold Laird Commercials, and later the Speedwings, were renown for the craftsmanship that went into them. The Speedwings were entirely custom-made to individual customer specifications, like a private yacht.

And the Lairds were fast. Matty Laird loved a good race and entered his airplanes aiming to win. Flown by Charles "Speed" Hollman and E. E. Ballaugh,

flew with an OX-5, which proved predictably underpowered because of the tapered wing's reduced surface area. Nevertheless, it confirmed that Meyers was on the right track. With a 220-horsepower J-5 Whirlwind the Taperwing was transformed into a thoroughbred.

It promptly won the 1928 National Air Race from New York to Los Angeles. Flown by famed racing pilot Johnny Livingston, it beat the highest performance competitor in its class, Matty Laird's Laird Solution piloted by one of Livingston's colorful rivals, Charles "Speed" Hollman.

The race was not without controversy. The participating machines were all supposed to be stock aircraft, but both the Taperwing Wacos and the Lairds were classifiable as nonproduction machines. The Wacos had a cleaned-up landing gear assembly and the Lairds had new wings. Several of the other contestants protested, but after some deliberation the organizers allowed the two types to participate. In any event, regardless of the other competitors, it was a race between the Taperwing and the Laird. The Taperwing's win achieved what Charlie Meyers had set out to do.

Over time, however, it wasn't the racing triumphs that gave the Taperwing its enduring reputation, but its stunning aerobatic performance. Its tapered wing's mass was more concentrated in its center than the

An excellent view of the Laird Commerical. After leaving Swallow Aircraft of Wichita, Kansas, in 1923 Laird specialized in custom building high-quality fast airplanes and air racers. He sold several Lairds to be used for airmail service because of their high speed. *Jim Koepnick/EAA*

Laird Commercials took first and second place in their class in the 1927 Spokane to Washington National Air Race. In the following year Hollman was a close second in his Laird to the Taperwing Waco from New York to Los Angeles, and he cleaned up in the subsequent free-for-all pylon races.

Matty Laird sold a number of Lairds as mail planes primarily because of their high cruise speed. The rest of his customers were the wealthy sportsman pilots who wanted what Matty advertised as "The Thoroughbred of the Air" and could afford his $10,000-plus price tag when a Whirlwind Waco was going for $7,300.

The design and production of open-cockpit biplanes weren't restricted to the usual suspects who had been long at the game from way before the pre-Lindbergh era. J. Don Alexander's timing with the Alexander Eaglerock couldn't have been better. Al Mooney had fixed the Eaglerock just in time for the Lindbergh craze, and it joined the Travel Airs and Wacos as one of the most successful open-cockpit biplanes of the Roaring Twenties. More than 900 Eaglerocks were made while the good times rolled. Like its two biggest competitors, the Alexander Airplane Company produced a large number of low-cost OX-5-powered airplanes but also got into the Whirlwind game and adopted other radials to its basic airframe as they became available.

Matty Laird advertised his airplane as The Thoroughbred of the Airways, conveying the custom-made quality and attention to performance. They weren't inexpensive, but attracted wealthy sports pilots.

The Travel Air 6000, seen here in Beryloid's art deco macaw color scheme, was the development of the Travel Air 5000, which won the Dole Derby to Hawaii in 1927 with stunt pilot Art Goebel in command. The 6000 was a foray into the regional airliner business.

© 1929

Travel Air &

Berryloid

AIRCRAFT FINISHES

International Orange, Travel Air Blue and Vesta Yellow—the colors of the brilliant Macaw, suggested the combination on this Travel Air

A more prosaically finished Travel Air 6000 being refueled by a Phillips fuel truck. The aircraft is owned by Phillips Petroleum and is being used for oblique aerial photography. The oil companies were big users of early corporate aircraft and found an increasingly lucrative market for aviation gasoline. *National Air and Space Museum*

And there were brand-new contenders galore, not particularly well-capitalized dreamers catching the Air Age wave with some credible airplanes. This was the time of the Kreider Reisner (a fine line of airplanes built by two men with previous ties to Waco), the American Eagle (run by Ed Porterfield), and the Pitcairn. Parks College built its own trainer, the Parks biplane.

In Tulsa, Oklahoma, Willis Brown and Waldo Emory, both in the mechanical instrumentation business and ex-Army pilots, formed the Mid-Continent Aircraft Company and designed the C-3 Spartan, yet another fine three-place, open-cockpit biplane, powered by a 128-horsepower Ryan Siemens air-cooled radial engine. The Spartan could have easily gone nowhere had it not been for yet another oil man, Bill Skelly, looking to invest his profits from the economic boom times. Why not the hot new field of aviation? Skelly acquired Mid-Continent for a cool million, which was real money back then. Soon C-3s were rolling out of the Spartan Aircraft Company's brand-new factory to serve the students of the Spartan School of Aeronautics. The type found a ready market beyond the school, with approximately 120 sold. Engine options included the 165-horsepower Curtiss Challenger and the Wright Whirlwind series.

And in Little Rock, Arkansas, a German engineer named Albert Voellmecke, who had worked for Heinkel in Germany, designed the Command Aire open-cockpit biplane. Built with the usual conventional construction techniques and initially powered by an OX-5, it was exceptionally stable. Command Aire's crazy test pilot, Wright "Ike" Vermilya, used to

demonstrate this desirable characteristic by climbing out of the cockpit in flight, straddling the fuselage like a horse, and steering by leaning left or right. Perhaps because of Vermilya's confidence-building antics, but more likely because they were good, competitively priced airplanes, several hundred Command Aires were sold with a variety of inline and radial engines.

As open-cockpit biplane madness took its course, the cabin monoplane was also making steady progress among personal-business aircraft, thanks in large measure to the efforts of Eddie Stinson and Clyde Cessna.

Stinson was having great success with the Detroiter biplane. Ten were delivered in 1926 when the company had been in production for less than half a year, and there was a strong backlog of orders. But Stinson was really a monoplane man, converted to the cause by having flown the big Junkers for years. He reasoned that with one efficient wing he could build a Detroiter that could haul a larger load than the SB-1 at a higher speed.

In April 1927 the first SM-1 (M stood for monoplane) took to the air and Stinson's predictions were confirmed. While its fuselage was essentially unchanged from the SB-1's, the new Detroiter was 10 miles faster and could haul 400 pounds more, powered by the same Wright Whirlwind. It was promptly entered in the 1927 Ford Reliability Tour and won hands down. Walter Beech was not participating that year because the date was changed and with some hard feeling he decided there wasn't sufficient time to prepare an entry. It is highly unlikely, however, that any Travel Air except a radical new design could have

SM-1 from Brunswick, Georgia, on a 4,600-mile non-stop solo flight to Rio de Janeiro, Brazil. He crossed the coast of Venezuela, headed out over the forbidding Amazon rain forest, and was never seen again.

In the same month a 23-year-old aspiring actress named Ruth Elder was attempting to become the first woman to cross the Atlantic in an airplane by retracing Lindbergh's route in an SM-1 named the *American Girl* with her pilot, George Haldeman. They ditched near a ship in the Azores and were treated by a sensation-hungry New York to a ticker tape parade anyway.

While Miss Elder and her companion were putting their flotation gear to good use, two Canadians vanished in an SM-1 over the Atlantic on a flight sponsored by the Carling Brewery, essentially on a mission to advertise beer. The following March a titled Englishwoman and her pilot vanished attempting an east to west crossing of the Atlantic (after having tricked Stinson into selling them an airplane by promising not to attempt the trip), and a Detroiter was ditched on the Greenland ice cap, its crew rescued by Eskimos.

Stinson was distressed by the toll that these senseless gimmick flights were taking on SM-1s and the image of aviation. To his great relief by the end of 1928 Lindbergh-itis seemed to have run its course. The only remaining stunt of note, one that shed a good light on the toughness of the Detroiter, was a local endurance flight in 1930. In a secondhand SM-1 named the *City of Chicago*, the Hunt brothers managed to remain airborne for a record 553 hours and 41 minutes on a flight that made them highly proficient in aerial refueling.

More important than the rash of gimmick flights in SM-1s was a steady stream of orders for them. In the first two years of production well over 100 of them were sold, a lucrative track record given their considerably higher price than the open-cockpit biplanes. The Detroiter's success prompted Stinson to conclude that the market was ready for a smaller cabin-class monoplane for business

Waco name confusion. The company started out as the Weaver Aircraft Company (Waco), so named by one of its founders, Buck Weaver. After Weaver left, the company name was changed to Advanced Aircraft Company, but the airplanes remained Wacos to honor Weaver's early support. Finally the company name was changed back to Waco to simplify life.

The Warner Scarab engines carved out a nice niche for themselves in the 110- to 165-horsepower range. The Scarabs appeared hard on the heels of the Wright Whirlwind that took personal aviation beyond the OX-5.

beaten Eddie Stinson and his Detroiter.

The Detroiter's victory and high load-carrying capacity made it a darling of all the Lindbergh wanna-bes in the world, which was a mixed blessing for Stinson, because several of these adventures ended badly. First in the air with the declared intent of circling the globe in 15 days was Ed Schlee (another oil man), owner of the Ford Reliability Tour winner, and his pilot, W. S. Brock. They painted *Pride of Detroit* in huge letters on the side of their airplane and after highly professional preparations flew to London uneventfully. Eighteen days and 145 hours of flying time after leaving North America they were in Tokyo, a remarkable achievement for a stock cabin-class airplane in 1927. There they wisely put the *Pride of Detroit* on a boat for the rest of the trip.

Other attempts in Detroiters at around the same time didn't turn out so well. Paul Redfern departed in an

The new Warner "Scarab" plant now in full operation is a model for the production of fine aircraft engines.

Completely equipped with the most modern and most efficient facilities —manned by specially trained and skilled aeronautical mechanics and engineers, the new Warner plant represents the finality in painstaking manufacturing procedure.

We believe it is fitting that the ideal light power plant should be made in the ideal factory.

110 H.P.   1850 R.P.M.
Weight 275 lbs.

WARNER "Scarab" ENGINES

WARNER AIRCRAFT CORPORATION · · · DETROIT, MICHIGAN

and pleasure. This led in 1928 to the introduction of the Stinson SM-2 Junior, which would evolve into one of the most outstanding personal cabin-class airplanes.

The Stinson Junior was initially a three- to four-place light cabin monoplane. It was the launch aircraft for the newly designed 110-horsepower Warner Scarab engine, and it looked like a mini-Detroiter. It was immediately popular, but its wealthy core clientele hankered for more performance and was willing to pay for it. In response the Junior was soon scaled up into a large cabin-class airplane equipped with a range of more powerful radials.

While Eddie Stinson was fretting over the stupid pilot tricks being performed in his SM-1s, Clyde Cessna was steadily progressing toward his goal of making a fully cantilevered cabin monoplane. His prototype, the sleek, bullet-shaped *Phantom*, was a creation of exquisite beauty, reminiscent in superficial appearance to Giuseppe Bellanca's efficient 1922 CF monoplane that won practically every race it entered but was never put in production.

The cantilevered wing was not only a stylish novelty for personal aircraft of the day, but a comparatively low drag structure that contributed to giving the *Phantom* outstanding performance in comparison to other airplanes for the power it had. Internal steel wire bracing provided torsional stiffness for the tapered wing.

Harking back to Cessna's earlier good experience with the Anzani engines and the lack of availability of better alternatives, the *Phantom* was powered by a 10-cylinder 90-horsepower Anzani radial. On the first flight in August 1927 it propelled the *Phantom* along at 100 miles per hour.

Following the good flight test results the *Phantom* was scaled up into the four-seat Model A, the series that came to be known as the Cessna cantilever monoplane. It established the type's basic airframe design for the remainder of the decade. The first Model A to be certified in August 1928 was the AA, which was equipped with a 120-horsepower Anzani. It performed well, but the French Anzani engine was problematic in terms of servicing and product support, prompting Cessna to search for an alternative. The Whirlwind was always a possibility (and would be used in limited numbers), but it made the airplane too expensive for a large segment of the market, and anyway, the whole point of the Cessna was equal performance with the most powerful biplanes of the day on half the horsepower.

The solution to Cessna's engine problem materialized when the 110-horsepower Warner Scarab appeared. The Scarab-equipped Cessna was certified as the AW. In

1928 the Cessna's arrival was dramatically announced when in the hands of Earl Rowland it won the New York–to–Los Angeles National Air Race in its class.

Earl Rowland's victory unleashed a deluge of orders for the Cessna cantilever monoplane, and Clyde Cessna had to scramble hard to raise the capital to expand production in new, bigger premises. But aviation was booming and on the strength of future orders investment funds were readily forthcoming as 1929 rolled around. In addition to the Successful A series of which approximately 300 would be produced in barely a year and a half, Cessna also introduced the 220-horsepower Whirlwind-powered BW rocketship and was planning to up the ante into the small airliner category.

The cabin-class airplane was slowly but steadily gaining ground during the second half of the 1920s. Other successful cabin-class designs joined the Stinsons and Cessnas on the flight line. Ryan capitalized on the Lindbergh connection with the Ryan Brougham, a five-seat commercialized version of the *Spirit of St. Louis*. At peak production as many as 20 Broughams were made per day.

Fairchild developed his FC cameraship into a series of successful large cabin monoplanes, including the F-71, used mostly by commercial operators but also favored by some corporations. And Curtiss introduced its only truly successful small airplane of the era, the three-seat cabin-class Curtiss Robin, available with the ancient OX-5 as well as a series of air-cooled

The Spartan Aircraft Company and School of Aeronautics symbol. The colorfully painted school aircraft used to embark on "dawn patrols" that became a school institution.

The Stinson SM Junior was a scaled-down version of the original Detroiter monoplane. The monoplane line was introduced by Stinson in 1927 with the SM-1. Initially using the same Wright Whirlwind as the Detroiter biplane, it was faster and could carry a higher load. In designing the four-to five-seat Junior, Stinson recognized the demand for a personal-business cabin monoplane as an alternative to the open biplanes. The SM-8A pictured here continues to haul sightseers over Cape Cod to earn its keep. It is powered by a 220-horsepower Lycoming.

radials. But one of the biggest cabin-class success stories was aimed at the lowest end of the market ignored by most manufacturers. It was Don Luscombe's Monocoupe, and it would become wildly popular as the weekend flyer's airplane of choice.

Unlike most makers of personal and business airplanes of the time, who got into the game because they saw potential in the profitable commercial uses for aircraft, Don Luscombe started out in aviation exclusively as a weekend pleasure flyer. On returning from France after World War I, Luscombe became a successful advertising executive in Davenport, Iowa, but he never forgot his rides in the Voisin over the idyllic French countryside. As soon as his means allowed, he learned to fly in a Jenny and purchased one with a partner. When his partner dunked the Jenny in the Mississippi River, Luscombe acquired a Laird Swallow on his own.

While he loved to fly, the thoroughly social Luscombe thought that tandem open-cockpit airplanes were completely useless for fun flying with friends. You were each so isolated in the separate open cockpits that you might as well be solo as far as any socializing was concerned. Luscombe became con-

Stinson Detroiter landing over a highway in the 1920s. Note how modern the airplane looks compared to the road traffic. *National Air and Space Museum*

The three-seat Curtiss Robin was the giant Curtiss conglomerate's entry into the light cabin class. It was intended to be an inexpensive personal airplane and was offered with the OX-5 engine as well as a variety of radials. It came late in the 1920s with the hope of cashing in on the Lindbergh craze (and realizing some success). *Kimm Anderson*

vinced that a very light side-by-side two-seater with an enclosed cabin was what the recreational aviation community needed to fly in a civilized fashion. He favored a high-wing monoplane to better see the landscape unfolding below. Inspired by the monoplane wing and the automobile industry's penchant to name sporting cars coupes, he named the airplane he envisioned the Monocoupe.

By mid-1926 Luscombe was at work building a mockup. His plan was to create what he saw as the best layout from the pilot's perspective and then get someone qualified to do the engineering. With the adman's panache, Luscombe talked his friends into financing what they considered to be his flighty pastime, and with the capital in hand the Central States Aero Company was formed in October 1926. Now all they needed was an airplane and someone to do the detailed design work and build it.

Luscombe had heard of a young farm boy named Clayton Folkerts who taught himself the basics of aircraft design and construction by building several of the flivver designs that were regularly featured in *Popular Mechanics*, complete with plans. He also taught himself the funda-

mentals of flying by hopping his better creations over the vast midwestern farmland. The two got together and a deal was struck. Folkerts became the Central States Aero Company's chief engineer.

The airframe that took shape under Folkerts' hand with Luscombe's advice looked like a cute cartoon plane that Felix the Cat would die to own. It had a steel tube fuselage and pushrods instead of cables for the controls, the Clark Y airfoil, and an all-moving tail. Its engine was a 60-horsepower Detroit Air Cat. It looked inspiring enough to entice Moline's airport manager to agree to test-fly it. In April 1927 it flew for the first time with few apparent vices.

The next big hurdle was obtaining the airplane's Approved Type Certificate under the new regulatory requirement. For that task Luscombe hired two New York University aeronautical engineering graduates, Jerome Lederer and Frederick Knack. The pair made few changes to Folkert's creation, documented the technical data, and in January 1928 the Monocoupe 22 was issued its ATC, well in time to benefit from the Lindbergh craze.

Dealers loved the brightly painted Monocoupes, which nicely complemented a biplane, such as the Waco 10, and a large cabin airplane, such as the Stinson Detroiter, to form a comprehensive product line. Only two drawbacks surfaced during the airplane's development: the familiar lack of capital and the lack of an engine more reliable than the cantankerous Air Cat (the Anzani and Siemens engines were also used but didn't prove to be much better).

Both problems were solved by Luscombe's association with Willard Velie Jr., son of the magnate behind the Velie automobiles. The smooth-talking Luscombe, the impressive little Monocoupe, and Velie Jr. soon had Velie Sr. in their corner. By the spring of 1928, Central States Aero had become the Moline, Illinois-based Mono-Aircraft subsidiary of the Velie Motors Corporation.

The Curtiss Robin's instrument panel was perfunctory but par for the course at the time. The old-fashioned turn and bank indicator in the upper center is a rare luxury. Clearly noticeable is the poor forward visibility on the ground resulting from the unfortunate combination of the bulky radial engine and the tail-wheel configuration.

The Stinson Detroiter's control yoke would have looked well on the bridge of any luxury motor yacht. Luxurious interior appointments were tempting for marketing reasons but difficult to realize because of weight considerations.

THE FLYING CARPET

The exploits of international long-distance record fliers in small personal airplanes during the 1920s and 1930s have been widely publicized. But missing out on the headlines were the adventures of a handful of sports pilots who flew their airplanes to the ends of the earth not to get into the record books or collect prize money, but merely to satisfy their own sense of adventure and curiosity. That was the goal of the pilots of the *Flying Carpet*.

The *Flying Carpet* was a Stearman C-3 purchased in 1931 by Richard Halliburton, a well-off American traveler, to take him around the world. When Halliburton bought the Stearman from a dealer in Los Angeles he knew nothing about airplanes and didn't know how to fly. He bought it, he wrote, because "it was love at first sight." He couldn't resist its rugged grace, its gold wings, and its lacquered red fuselage—and the dealer told him it would do everything he asked of it.

Halliburton's next step was to find a pilot. It didn't take him long. Moye Stevens, recently out of Stanford University and hauling passengers from Los Angeles back and forth across the Rockies for a local airline, readily agreed that a round-the-world trip in a Stearman was just the ticket.

The pair winged their way across the United States on a shakedown flight plagued with engine trouble. In New York the engine was worked on for three weeks. When all was in order at last, they crossed the Atlantic with the *Flying Carpet* to France the smart way—on a luxury ocean liner.

A brief homage to Paris and then the adventure began in earnest. They were off to, as it was then called, Timbuctoo. "I've always wanted to go there," wrote Halliburton. They could have followed the west coast of Africa

and the Niger River inland, but they chose the Little Prince's route straight across the Sahara's forbidding sands.

They reached the Beau Geste fort of Colomb-Béchar by the skin of their teeth in a raging sand storm and consorted with Foreign Legionnaires for six days until it passed. In the deepest Sahara they were amazed to find a chain of Shell Oil Company self-service aviation gasoline depots that they could access with a key given to them by the Foreign Legion. For endless hours they droned across the sand taking turns at the controls (Halliburton was becoming an accomplished pilot), and when at last the Niger River came into view they turned east and followed it into Timbuktu.

They found a sprawling community of dusty mud dwellings and mosques that had seen their better days, a place more foreign than the remotest village is today—and for Halliburton a boyhood dream realized. On the trip back to Paris for an overhaul before heading for Asia, they nearly lost their hearts to a dancer in the ancient Moroccan city of Fez, continuing their journey only after a long delay and with great reluctance.

It was adventure upon adventure when they set the *Flying Carpet*'s compass on "E" for east after the overhaul. A duel with the Matterhorn (they won), bird's-eye views of St. Mark's in Venice, the Haghia Sophia in Istanbul, the Dome of the Rock in Jerusalem, the pyramids outside Cairo, giving Prince Ghazi of Iraq a ride in the *Flying Carpet* (he bought a Spartan Executive when he became king), slow rolling over the Taj Mahal, meeting by chance the engaging young German aviatrix Elly Beihorn on her way to Australia solo in her 80-horsepower Klemm monoplane, a duel with Mt. Everest (they lost), and the shrunken heads of Borneo.

On their wanderings around Borneo (the *Flying Carpet* was on floats by now) they befriended a Dayak chief who presented them with 12 shrunken heads as a parting gift. To Stephens' horror Halliburton felt compelled to keep them. Soon they were beset by calamities, including a violent typhoon, a sunken log in their landing path that nailed a pontoon, and even a cloud of locusts over the Philippines that nearly brought down the *Flying Carpet*. Stephens blamed their bad luck on the heads and convinced Halliburton to part with a few every time disaster struck. Lo and behold, after the last head went overboard it was smooth flying all the way to Manila.

And there the aerial adventure ended. The *Flying Carpet* and her crew embarked on the SS *President McKinley* and sailed for San Francisco, well over a year after they had set out. They didn't just build magical airplanes back then. Some also knew how to travel in them.

The Flying Carpet
over the Taj Mahal.

The Cessna B series monoplane, which differed from the A series by being equipped with the more powerful 220-horsepower J-4 Wright Whirlwind engine. A real rocket ship, it was not built in large numbers because the whole point of the Cessnas was to do on 110 horsepower what competing aircraft did on 220 horsepower. *National Air and Space Museum*

A Cessna AW rounds a pylon at one of the National Air Races. Cessnas were very successful at pylon racing because of their efficient airframes. *National Air and Space Museum*

The six-seat Cessna CW-6 exhibited at the 1929 Wichita Automobile Show. The CW-6, powered by a 225-horsepower Wright Whirlwind, was to be Cessna's next step to getting into airliner manufacturing, but became a casualty of the Great Depression. *National Air and Space Museum*

No time was lost in bringing the parent company's formidable resources to bear on the engine problem. The result was the five-cylinder 60-horsepower Velie M-5, a greatly improved Air Cat. The Velie-powered Monocoupe received an airframe face-lift and was certified as the Model 70. Monocoupe was set to claim the very light cabin class entirely for itself. By the end of 1928 Mono-Aircraft had sold 278

Monocoupes, an achievement right up there with the results of any major manufacturer.

The Velie association didn't last long for Mono-Aircraft. Velie Sr. died suddenly of a heart attack. Overwhelmed by the management responsibilities that befell him, Velie Jr. decided that the best solution was to sell everything (and then, he too, died). Mono-Aircraft was bought by Allied Aviation, a group of St.

Clyde Cessna in the Phantom. Cessna designed and built the Phantom after he left Travel Air in 1926. It was his proof-of-concept prototype for Cessna's fully cantilevered-wing monoplane. From this airplane he developed the A series Cessnas that quickly acquired a reputation for speed on low power. *National Air and Space Museum*

The General Aristocrat was a three-seat cabin design from the General Airplanes Corporation of Buffalo, New York. Introduced in 1929, it was a casualty of the Depression, notwithstanding Lady Mary Heath's rousing endorsement. Its designer, J. Francis Arcier, moved on to Waco, where one of his first projects was the development of the first cabin Waco, the QDC. This only surviving example of the General Aristocrat is owned by the Antique Airplane Museum in Blakesburg, Iowa.

OPPOSITE: The Aeronca Bathtub was an ultralight so-called "flivver plane" in development by 1928–1929. It was seen as a source of low-cost flying during the Depression. Pictured is the two-seat C-3, originally powered by a two-stroke 36-horsepower Aeronca engine. It enjoyed considerable popularity, staying in production through 1933. It was the ancestor of an entire line of Aeroncas, including the Chief.

Louis investors who also owned Lambert Engines. Luscombe remained in charge of Mono-Aircraft, but the Velie powerplants became Lamberts.

Monocoupe developed two other models around this time. One was the large cabin-class 220-horsepower Wright J-5–powered Monocoach, which was shut out of the market by the Stinson Detroiter. The other was the Monosport, a scaled-up Monocoupe powered by 100 to 110 horsepower Kinner and Warner engines. It became the darling of the air-racing community, reaping great rewards in all kinds of highly modified racing versions. But the most popular type continued to be the diminutive Monocoupe.

As the 1920s drew to a close, the frenzied drive to have fun above all else was reaching its peak. Several small airplanes appeared in the spirit of the Monocoupe, intended to be flown primarily for fun. Two interesting small biplanes aimed at the sports flying market were the Arrow Sport and the Great Lakes biplane.

The tiny taper-winged Arrow Sport was unusual for a biplane in two respects. It had side-by-side seating for the pilot and one passenger, and it had two cantilevered wings, which eliminated the need for struts between them. Designer Swen Swenson, however, had to include struts after all, because pilots felt uncom-

As aircraft got more complex, so did the accessory equipment, including the sensitive carburetor. It may have contributed to easier starting, but not as much as the starter motors that were then coming into use.

The Aeronca C-2 was the precursor of the slightly more capable C-3. In this picture it is being tried out by the colorful air show and record pilot, Roscoe Turner. Note the simple braking mechanism at the top of the wheel. *National Air and Space Museum*

OPPOSITE: The Savoia Marchetti was the ultimate aerial toy. It was a diminutive Italian amphibian, powered by a 100-horsepower Kinner engine, and produced under license in limited quantities in America. Its rather ineffective water rudder made its aquatic operations more of an art than handling the usual seaplane. *Kimm Anderson*

fortable without them. The Arrow was underpowered with a 60-horsepower LeBlond engine, but it became considerably peppier with a 100-horsepower Kinner. The Arrow Sport got a late start and only about 80 were built until the 1920s abruptly stopped roaring.

Contrary to the Arrow Sport, the tandem Great Lakes biplane, which was another latecomer that appeared in 1929, became an all-time favorite. It was even put back in production with a modern Lycoming as late as the early 1980s. It was small for its time, aimed at the sport aerobatic pilot, and was powered by a 90- to 95-horsepower inline American Cirrus engine of British origin to minimize drag. Unusual for the time was the Great Lakes' use of stamped aluminum wing ribs. Otherwise its construction was conventional. Later models had a larger vertical stabilizer. The Great Lakes was a sports aerobatic pilot's delight and managed to hang on until 1933.

One of the most unusual open-cockpit biplanes of the Roaring Twenties for the pilot out to have sheer fun was the tiny three-place Savoia-Marchetti amphibian. An Italian airplane license produced in limited numbers in the United States, it had a speed boat–like fuselage and was powered by a 100-horsepower Kinner on which it could buzz around at about 85 miles per hour. There was no better way to

Introduced in 1929, the Great Lakes was a recreational biplane, small for its time and delightfully agile. Powered by a small, 90- to 95-horsepower inline Cirrus engine, it also looked sleek compared to its peers. The Depression finally claimed it in 1933, but its aerobatic prowess coaxed investors to attempt to revive it for limited production runs as late as the 1980s (re-engined with a Lycoming flat-four engine).

Fairchild's first open-cockpit biplanes were really Kreider Reisners. Fairchild sought to expand its product line beyond its utility cabin monoplane and did so by buying Kreider Reisner in 1929. The biplanes, which were contemporaries of the Travel Air, Waco, and Eaglerock, didn't remain in production for long. Fairchild used its Kreider Reisner division to develop the Fairchild 24 cabin monoplane.

make a splash at your Long Island country club than by buzzing the golf course, landing on Long Island Sound, and taxiing up the boat ramp onto the lawn for tea. But you had better watch the regulations. The New York City Police Department flew several S-56s on an aerial beat.

As the stock market soared and personal-business air-planes became big business, big business was paying attention. For some of the dominant light airplane makers, 1929 was the year to make deals. Curtiss and Wright agreed to merge that year and made Walter Beech an offer for Travel Air that he couldn't refuse. Stinson became part of the E. L. Cord empire, which included Lycoming Motors and the Cord, Duesenberg, and Auburn automo-bile companies. It would later own American Airlines. Stearman was bought by United Aircraft, owner of Boeing, Pratt and Whitney, Hamilton Standard, and United Airlines. It wouldn't be long before the acquired companies would be especially thankful for their fate.

On October 16, 1929, ATC 257 was issued to the Waco CTO, a Taperwing model powered by the 220-horsepower Wright Whirlwind J-6 engine. It was the last ATC to be issued before Black Tuesday, the October 29 collapse of the stock market that triggered the Great Depression.

The Pietenpol Air Camper was a
flivver plane of the Depression era.
Its plans were made available in
Popular Mechanics, and it continued
to be built by home builders long
after the Depression and even
World War II. A challenge was to
find a reliable engine for it. This Air
Camper is an original 1930s model.
Its water-cooled engine looks like it
would be more at home on a
Victorian motor launch.

Jim Koepnick/EAA

The most immediate effect of the stock-market crash on the makers of personal-business aircraft was a drastic reduction, but not a total collapse, of back orders and new business. There were some businesses and wealthy individuals who hadn't been heavily invested in the stock market and continued to have capital, even to buy airplanes. It would take until 1932 for the shock of the crash to work its way through the economy and drag the country to the depths of the Depression. In the meantime, the aircraft makers instituted severe cutbacks and those that could started living off capital in the hopes of not running out before a turnaround. Most manufacturers that didn't have deep-pocketed parent companies or wealthy backers didn't make it.

In a desperate bid to survive, many companies turned to making light, bargain-priced aircraft powered by 25- to 40-horsepower engines, the so-called flivver planes. This became the era of the flivvers: the American Eaglet, the Alexander Flyabout, the Cessna EC-1 and -2, the Heath Parasol, and the Buhl Pup, all selling for $1,500 or a lot less. *Popular Mechanics* urged its readers to build the ultralight Pietenpol Air Camper, and many did. The wealthy Rae Rearwin who entered the aviation field with the larger Ken Royce biplane in early 1929 came out with the tiny Junior.

Perhaps the best remembered of the flivver planes are the Aeronca C-2 and C-3, the so-called Flying Bathtubs. They were already on the way when the Depression struck, so they got a head start over most of the competition; but astute marketing also helped. Its maker, the Cincinnati, Ohio-based Aeronautical Corporation of America managed to get famed aviators Jimmy Doolittle and Roscoe Turner to commend the little airplanes.

The C-2 was a 25-horsepower single-seater introduced in 1929. The C-3 was a marginally more refined 36-horsepower two-seater that appeared in 1931. A popular airplane that was practically a toy, the C-3 remained in production through 1933. It evolved into the Chief and the rest of the much-loved Aeroncas that would be made by the thousands.

This was also the time when another ultra-light airplane that would become a household name had its beginnings, although it, too, was under development prior to the Depression. It was the creation of C. Gilbert Taylor of Rochester, New York. In 1927 and 1928 Taylor and his brother, Gordon, designed the two-seat side-by-side parasol-winged Chummy, powered alternatively by a 90-horsepower Anzani, a 113-horsepower Siemens, and a 90-horsepower Kinner in the quest for the nonexistent perfect small radial. Its engine wasn't its only problem, however. The Chummy was an all-around dog. Tragically, it killed Gordon Taylor.

After Gordon's death and the onset of the Depression, Gilbert Taylor moved to Bradford, Pennsylvania, in part to get away and in part enticed by a generous financial offer by the city's leading businessmen interested in attracting an aviation business. Among the investors from Bradford was yet another oil man

OPPOSITE, LEFT AND ABOVE: The fat Gee Bee Bullets made by the Granville Brothers of Springfield, Massachusetts, mesmerized the air-racing crowds eager for entertainment in the depths of the Depression. Today Delmar Benjamin's replica Gee Bee thrills the crowds and proves that in the hand of a master it is a pussycat.

Don Luscombe's entry into the personal airplane market, the first Monocoupe. Designed by Clayton Folkerts, a self-taught aeronautical engineer, it was built entirely for recreational flying. It became a great success, thanks in part to Luscombe's outstanding selling skills. Funding came from the Velie family, owners of the Velie Motors Corporation. Velie custom developed the early Monocoupe's 60-horsepower engine. *National Air and Space Museum*

OPPOSITE: Matty Laird's personal Laird Commercial, holding for takeoff, flown by its restorer, Ken Love.

The flying wires on an airplane are a crucial structural bracing component. They can snap in flight so must be carefully inspected for looseness and knicks.

named William T. Piper. Shortly after Taylor moved to Bradford, he went bankrupt. Piper bought the company from the receiver for $761 and gave half to Taylor in a partnership to start over. The two decided that in view of market conditions a flivver design was their best bet to weather the storm. It was not an auspicious beginning for the airplane that would become the Piper Cub and would go on to a production run exceeding 21,000 airplanes.

Not everyone turned to the minimalist flivver approach to survive. Many highly skilled designers and pilots hoped to weather the hard times by turning to air racing in a big way. Some money could always be raised to fund one souped-up airplane, and hundreds of thousands flocked to the air meets to be entertained for a few pennies. The pilots who took the top cash prizes could make a handsome living (or blow it all preparing for the next meet). While already reasonably well established in prior years, it was during the Depression that air racing really came into its own.

In the end many companies were beyond salvation. Grimly they clutched at every straw, some for years, as orders slowed to a trickle, and then quietly vanished. Practically none of the companies that manufactured open-cockpit biplanes exclusively made it. Alexander, American Eagle, Command Aire all shut their doors. Travel Air was absorbed into the Curtiss Wright organization and essentially disappeared. Cessna, laden with debt for the anticipated expansion before the Crash, mothballed its facilities.

Others hung on by the skin of their teeth. Skelly Oil kept Spartan barely alive through its School of Aeronautics. Waco retrenched and placed its hopes in Clayt Bruckner's management skills. Mono-Aircraft was heading for turbulence. Stinson, Fairchild, and Stearman were relying on the strength of conglomerates and benefactors to make it through.

Cruel as the Depression was to the personal-business aircraft industry, there would be survivors. And in a surprisingly short time they would play leading roles in a robust revival that would come to be known as the golden age of aviation.

The All American Aircraft Show was a major annual industry trade event. In 1928 art deco was king and the twenties were roaring.

OPPOSITE: A Ryan Brougham at the Ryan plant in San Diego sometime after Lindbergh's flight when the company was cashing in on the fame the trip garnered. Note how closely it resembles the *Spirit of St. Louis*. Where this airplane has cockpit windows Lindbergh had the extra gas tank, behind metal skin that completely eliminated any forward visibility, except by periscope. *via Karl Stauffer*

Louise Thaden being wheeled into the winner's circle in her Travel Air 4000 after winning the first transcontinental Women's Air Derby in 1929. Her Travel Air was the first to have a NACA cowl, earning it the name Speedwing. Thaden prevailed over competitors including Amelia Earhart, Pancho Barnes, Blanche Noyes, and Ruth Nichols over the 2,759-mile course. *National Air and Space Museum*

The only surviving air-worthy Cessna AW. Its claim to fame was the internally braced cantilever wing, an obsession of Clyde Cessna's that he realized perfectly. He must have gone nuts when all those struts started showing up on the Cessnas after World War II. *Ted Koston/EAA*

The product line of an aircraft dealer reveals the available choices. This dealer has all the bases covered with the large-cabin Brougham, the small-cabin Monocoupe, and the open-cockpit Waco 10.

Knapp Flying Service, Inc.
Distributors for

RYAN Five-Place Brougham — Sistership to Lindbergh's "Spirit of St. Louis"

ALL ON
EXHIBIT AT
ALL-AMERICAN
AIRCRAFT
SHOW

Two-Place MONO COUPE
Quiet-Comfortable-All Enclosed-Safe
The Individual Plane of the Future.

Three-place WACO 10
The Largest Selling Airplane Made
(55 Sold in Michigan to date)

Flying Instruction
On new types of planes only—including Wright-motored planes
Both Cabin and Open Cockpit Types

CROSS COUNTRY TAXI TRIPS IN WHIRLWIND-ENGINED PLANES
Airplane and Motor Repair—Prompt Service by Experienced Men

WE HAVE ON HAND VARIOUS MODELS OF THE AIRPLANES WE SELL
and will gladly demonstrate at any time — *Anywhere in Michigan*

KNAPP FLYING SERVICE, INC.
Ypsilanti Airport—Ypsilanti, Michigan   Phone - Ypsilanti 7143F13
EDWARD G. KNAPP   M. E. OLIPHANT   RICHARD F. YOUNG

You never knew who would be swinging your prop at a top air race. Charles Lindbergh helping to start a de Havilland Moth at the 1928 National Air Races. *National Air and Space Museum*

CHAPTER 4

Cabin Class Supreme

It required an optimism that few people possessed to see any future for the personal aircraft industry as the Depression tightened its grip on the economy in the aftermath of the Great Crash. Between 1929 and 1934 the number of companies making airplanes diminished from 132 to 48. The number of engine makers declined from 21 to 10 during the same period. In 1929 aircraft manufacturers produced 6,193 civilian airplanes. In 1932 they made only about 550. Although these numbers are bleak, they also show that while the industry was down it was by no means out.

Stinson and Waco, two of the most prolific makers of personal airplanes, were both survivors. Both companies had low debt and inventory levels, key factors in being able to severely cut back operations and remain in business. Stinson managed to squeak by thanks, in part, to support from its newly acquired and well-capitalized corporate parent, E. L. Cord. Waco owed its survival in large measure to Clayton Bruckner's highly disciplined, conservative financial management.

While Eddie Stinson, Clayton Bruckner, and most of their contemporaries were struggling to keep their companies in business, another well-known aircraft industry executive, Walter Beech, found himself in an unusual position. He had become modestly wealthy and had no company of his own to worry about. Beech's share of the profits from the sale of Travel Air to Curtiss Wright was estimated to be approximately a million dollars when the deal closed. Much of this amount was in Curtiss Wright stock, which plummeted from $30 a share when Travel Air was sold to 75 cents a share by 1932. But Beech must have cashed in sometime before the stock completely collapsed because he was able to quit his executive position with Curtiss Wright in 1932 to establish Beechcraft from his own resources and fund the development of the airplane that would bring him lasting fame, the Staggerwing.

Stinson, Waco, and Beechcraft were among the biggest competitors at the upper end of the personal and corporate aircraft industry as the recovery from the Depression slowly got under way. Along with Howard and Spartan, they transformed the 1930s into the golden age of the large cabin-class airplane.

While the Cessna Aircraft Company closed its doors and Curtiss retired the Robin, Stinson pressed on with the SM series. In 1930, the company reacted to the Depression by introducing a competitively priced version of the Junior, the SM-8A, powered by a nine-cylinder 215-horsepower Lycoming radial. It offered everything found in aircraft in the $10,000 price range, such as a soundproofed cabin, cabin heat, electric engine starter, wheel brakes, and even a parking brake, yet it cost only $5,775. Stinson's aggressive pricing paid off in

The QDC's engine shown without its ring cowl. Even with the ring cowl installed, the engine was not nearly as well cowled as the radials on later aircraft would be when the low-drag NACA cowl came into common use. Still, the QDC cruised at 100 miles per hour on 165 horsepower with four in cabin-class comfort for up to four hours.

The SM 5 Stinson Jr. was the first version of the smaller Stinson cabin-class Detroiters aimed at the persona-business flying community. Early Juniors three- to four-seat aircraft powered by a 110-horsepower Warner Scarab engine, which was quickly upgraded to a variety of engines of higher horsepower because of the market's demand for more performance. The airframe was also enlarged to a four- to five-seat version.

Waco proudly announced its entry into the cabin-class market, stressing economy, short field performance, and the link to the highly popular open-cockpit F series. The cabin Waco sold well in spite of the Depression.

volume sales. More than 350 SM-8As were sold in 1930 in spite of the challenging economic conditions.

It looked as if Stinson's SM series would have the cabin-class field largely to itself. But in a little under a year, with the economy still in a distressing downward spiral, the company suddenly found itself facing a feisty competitor. It was the Waco QDC, the first in a new line of aircraft from the biplane maker in Troy, Ohio, that would become known as the Cabin Waco.

By the late 1920s Waco began to realize that in view of the trends in the personal-business aircraft industry, and Stinson's success with the SB and SM series, it needed to make a cabin airplane to remain fully competitive. In developing its first production entry into the cabin class, the company followed its traditional path of relying heavily on its current models to bring out a new design.

The basis for the QDC was the Model F, Waco's latest open-cockpit biplane. In the Model F, Waco

sought to broaden its market share by keeping the airplane's price down without sacrificing traditional Waco performance. Bruckner and his colleagues achieved this objective by opting for a relatively low-cost and low-powered engine, a 110-horsepower Warner Scarab, and designing an airframe for it that was considerably lighter and aerodynamically cleaner than earlier Waco airframes. The strategy worked. The RNF, as it was called under Waco's coding system, became an instant best seller with more than 150 sold through 1931.

To create the QDC, A. Francis Arcier, Waco's chief engineer who had recently arrived from the General Aircraft Company where he designed the Aristocrat cabin monoplane, used the Model F airframe as his point of departure and re-engineered it into an enclosed four-place design. The tail and landing gear were retained unchanged, the wing was slightly modified, the fuselage was widened and extended to the upper wings to form the cabin, and the seven-cylinder 165-horsepower Continental was chosen for the engine.

The junction of the upper wing and the fuselage was novel for a cabin biplane—until then the usual layout had been an independent upper wing supported by struts. But the new design was logical given the need for the enclosed cabin space and simplicity of construction, and it was borrowed from the layout of a typical high-wing cabin monoplane.

Unveiled at the 1931 Detroit Air Show, the QDC was well received. In the Waco tradition it had excel-

lent short field takeoff and landing characteristics, and its robust construction suited it well for operating from the many rough grass and dirt strips of the day. The cozy, upholstered cabin made you feel as if you were sitting in your family car.

For pilots accustomed to being strapped into a breezy, open cockpit behind the wings, the enclosed cabin must have been downright serene, and the visi-

A strong effort was made to finish the QDC's cabin in an automotive style to convey a sense of luxury. Note the handles for rolling down the windows. The throw-over yoke was a common feature on cabin-class airplanes of the 1930s.

The Stinson Reliant was the next step up for Stinson from the Detroiter series. It was based on the Model R, which was developed in late 1931 by Bob Ayer, co-designer of the Gee Bee racers, who was hired specifically to give the Detroiter more speed. The SR-5, powered by a 225-horsepower Lycoming radial, was the first Reliant to sell in quantity. This Canadian Reliant is shown still hard at work in the 1970s and 1980s. *Antique Airplane Association*

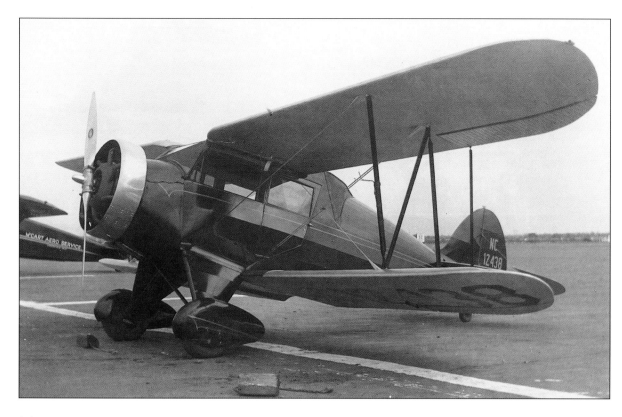

bility was in some ways also an improvement, helped by the skylight above the pilots' seats. A set of triangular windows extending aft of the cabin gave good visibility toward the rear, an uncommon luxury in cabin airplanes. The shape that these aft windows gave the fuselage prompted some to dub the airplane the Humpback Waco.

The QDC wasn't going to win any speed dashes, but it was a reliable airplane and had no nasty handling surprises. It would drone along at about 100 miles per hour in cruise burning a very economical (by the standards of the day) 10 gallons per hour for up to four hours on its 40-gallon fuel supply. Its performance was only marginally lower than that of the Stinson SM-8A Junior, and at $5,885 it was competitively priced.

The following year Waco brought out an improved version of its cabin biplane, the UEC, upgrading the engine to a 210-horsepower Continental without increasing the price. The 1933 model, the UIC, incorporated many small refinements including a roomier cabin, longer fuselage, and redesigned, faired-in wrap-around rear windows. The most notable change was a sleek, deep chord NACA cowling around the 210-horsepower Continental with aerodynamic blisters over the rocker arm boxes and a recontoured forward fuselage section to match. The UIC also sported streamlined

wheelpants. The modifications added 15 miles per hour to cruise speed, and fuel capacity was increased to 70 gallons to leverage the extra speed. In spite of these improvements, the price was increased by only $100.

Waco was in the cabin class to stay, and the market took note. The UIC sold briskly to individuals and corporations alike. Jackie Cochran, Felix Dupont Jr., Champion Spark Plug Company, Skelly Oil, and Texaco were among the customers for the airplane.

Eddie Stinson responded swiftly to the pressure put on the Stinson Junior by the Waco QDC. For the 1931 model year he renamed the SM-8A the Model S and slashed its price to $4,995. Simultaneously Stinson embarked on a project to take the SM series to the next level in its evolution. A major upgrade transformed it into the Stinson R, which refined into the SR Reliant. The Reliant would put the company in a good position to hold its own in the face of increased competition from Waco—or anyone else.

What Stinson was chiefly looking for out of the mature SM Junior design was more speed. When company test pilot and salesman Jack Kelley was weathered in at Granville Brothers Aircraft in Springfield, Massachusetts, home of the famed Gee Bee racers, he saw an opportunity to set in motion the Junior's upgrade while talking to designers Bob Hall and Bob

The cabin Waco quickly evolved from the QDC. In 1935 Waco divided its cabin-class line to a standard and a custom model. The custom-cabin Waco was made to order with the most luxurious appointments. The five-seat YKS-7 with a 225-horsepower Jacobs L4 engine was the 1937 standard model, in production for several years. The Waco pictured is a 1939 YKS-7 model.

The Custom Waco (YKC) was made to detailed individual customer specifications. Note the analogy to the luxury automobile.

THE *Plus* OF WACO OWNERSHIP...

• The Waco owner forfeits none of the advantages that attend owner-ship of the finest automobile. Waco seats are luxuriously comfortable, and cabins are generously spacious—licensed for five persons . . . Waco performance satisfies the most crit-ical demands . . . And Waco offers the benefits of world-wide sales and service facilities approached by no other airplane manufacturer. Your local dealer will welcome an oppor-tunity to demonstrate.

Waco Leads in Aircraft Registration

WACO
AIRPLANES
THE WACO AIRCRAFT COMPANY
TROY • OHIO

JUNE 1937

Ayer. He managed to convince Ayer, who was work-ing for Granville at no salary, to join Stinson and see what he could make of the Junior (Hall would follow Ayer to Stinson a year later).

Ayer gave the airplane an aerodynamic cleanup by shortening the fuselage, reducing its weight, and installing a low-drag cowl. The gear was changed to a semicantilevered design similar to the gear on the Gee Bee Sportsters and was carefully faired in. The gear lay-out was suitable for being upgraded to retractable gear, which was planned for a future version of the airplane. While the emphasis was on aerodynamics, increased passenger comfort was also taken into consideration, and the fuselage was raised to provide more cabin space.

With the aerodynamic cleanup, the Model R ended up being about 10 miles per hour faster than the Model S with the same 215-horsepower Lycoming engine. To further differentiate the two airplanes, Stinson decided to position the Model R as a deluxe executive airplane and equipped it with a suitably plush, soundproofed cabin. It was an elegant airplane, looking every bit the executive limousine compared to the workhorse appearance of the Model S. Its price tag was $1,000 higher than its predecessor's.

Eddie Stinson was pleased with the Model R, and on January 25, 1932, the day it was issued its ATC, he took it on its maiden sales tour. His first stop was Chicago's Municipal Airport where he flew demon-stration hops into the early evening. It was already dark when he took off on the last flight of the day with a steel company CEO and two of his associates and headed out over Lake Michigan.

They had just passed over the lakeshore when the Lycoming sputtered for a moment and then abruptly quit. Stinson set up for an emergency landing on the beach but elected during the descent to try for the Jackson Park golf course instead. He just about had the course made when with a terrific bang the air-plane's right wing slammed into the facility's giant flag pole, lurking invisibly in the darkness.

The mortally wounded airplane cartwheeled into the ground, but its fuselage remained intact and there was no fire. It appeared that the occupants, though badly bruised, got away without critical injuries. Eddie Stinson was taken to Illinois Central Hospital with broken ribs and walked unassisted into the emergency admissions room, but there he collapsed, and by the next morning he was dead.

There was a tremendous outpouring of grief from the aviation community, for Stinson was universally liked. At his funeral, attended by thousands, Jimmy

Doolittle flew overhead. The Stinson factory's devastated employees suddenly found themselves facing an uncertain future. The Depression was still deepening, and the company had become rudderless. Production plummeted to less than 50 aircraft during 1932 (about 30 of them Model Rs), but massive salary cuts kept the employees on the payroll.

Slowly, management rallied under the guidance of Bill Mara and chief engineer Jack Irvine, and by fall the company had a retractable gear version of the Model R flying, the R-3. It was graceful for its time, but the speed gains realized by the retractable gear were disappointing.

The aesthetic appeal of retractable gear is irresistible to some designers, but the fact is that on light aircraft designed to fly at speeds of approximately 150 miles per hour or less, the extra weight of the costly retraction mechanism negates most of the drag reduction achieved. A simple, inexpensive well-faired-in fixed gear is the better option. This was the conclusion of Stinson's executives, and by the spring of 1933 the company had bounced back from the loss of Eddie Stinson with the introduction of a new fixed-gear air-

plane that would become a best seller. It was the Stinson SR Reliant.

The Reliant was a refinement of the basic design of the Model R. It was equipped with an attractive, new cantilever landing gear that gave it a wider wheelbase. It also had a slightly redesigned wing and vertical stabilizer, an improved, low-drag NACA cowl, and benefited from many stylistic enhancements. The original SR retained the 215-horsepower engine, but the SR-2, approved simultaneously under the same ATC, came with a 240-horsepower Lycoming. Over 100 Reliants were sold in 1933, including the custom SR-1 and SR-3 (two of each built) and the SR-4 (one built), which varied from the original Reliant only in minor ways.

In spring 1934 Stinson brought out the SR-5. It got a small but significant power boost from an engine upgrade to a 225-horsepower Lycoming and a sleeker NACA nose cowl. It was also the first production airplane in its class to be equipped with flaps, or, as Stinson called them, Selectiv-Glide speed arresters. A popular version of the airplane was the SR-5A, which was equipped with a more powerful 245-horsepower Lycoming. With the SR-5 series, Stinson was solidly back in business.

The Beech Staggerwing is the uncrowned king of the large cabin class. Walter Beech aimed for the highest executive segment of the corporate market when he and Ted Wells left Curtiss Aircraft to form Beechcraft in 1932, explicitly to build the Staggerwing. Note the negative stagger of the wings that gave the airplane its popular name. Wells designed this configuration to give the pilot better overhead and lateral visibility. The pictured model is a 450-horsepower Pratt and Whitney–powered D17S, the most numerous Staggerwing built, including 412 for the U.S. armed forces for liaison duty in World War II. *Carl Schuppel/EAA*

The first Staggerwing ever built, the Model B17R. Powered by a 420-horsepower Wright, it first flew on November 5, 1932, and shortly exceeded 200 miles per hour in sustained level flight. It proved too expensive for the market at $18,000 and was scaled down into the 225-horsepower B17L with retractable gear, which was the first of the production Staggerwings.

While Stinson and Waco were skillfully fishing for the price/performance combination that would profitably net the greatest number of buyers still able and willing to spend money on airplanes in the aftermath of the Crash, Walter Beech had settled on a different strategy. He reasoned that at the very top of the economic pyramid was a potential clientele of business executives rich to the point of being Depression-proof. If they were offered a personal business airplane of the highest performance and quality, they couldn't resist it and would have the resources to snap it up.

Behind the intense, stoical expression that made Walter Beech look more like an accountant than a pilot, he was a speed demon. Few of his accomplishments gave him the kind of personal sense of satisfaction that he derived from the achievements of the 200-plus-mile-per-hour Travel Air Mystery Ship. As he pondered the future at Curtiss Wright he reasoned that if he could create a four- to five-seat executive airplane as fast as the Mystery Ship and as luxurious as the most exquisite limousine, it would be a sure winner. It would also be an airplane that would have double the performance of the typical cabin-class airplane of the time.

The aircraft that Beech had on his mind in 1932 began to take form a year earlier when a young engineer at Curtiss Wright named Ted Wells started working on its design. Wells had been hired by Travel Air in 1929 after he graduated from Princeton with a degree in mechanical engineering. He was also a pilot who had learned to fly in a

Louise Thaden (left) and her copilot Blanche Noyes with the 420-horsepower C17R Staggerwing they piloted to victory in the 1936 Bendix Trophy race from New York to Los Angeles. It was the first year women were allowed to compete, and they came in first and second, with Laura Ingalls, flying a Lockheed Orion, placing second after Thaden and Noyes. Thaden flew the stock Staggerwing (except for extra fuel tanks) in economy cruise and beat many aircraft built especially for racing. Thaden's victory was a powerful demonstration of the capabilities of production personal aircraft.

This dramatic portrait of a Staggerwing shows the streamlined and faired frontal area and the gear retraction mechanism. It hints at the challenges of maintaining directional control in face of the powerful radial engine, given the relatively narrow wheelbase. *National Air and Space Museum*

Jenny and had barnstormed during the summers of his college years in an OX-powered Travel Air.

Like Beech, Wells was bitten by the speed bug, and in 1930 on his own time he had designed and built a racing biplane powered by a 200-horsepower Wright radial, which he called the Wells Special. Although it was a private project it was also officially designated as the Travel Air Model W4B. The Wells Special had a short career. Soon after it was completed it experienced aileron flutter at 500 feet on a high-speed pass and broke up. Amazingly, Wells managed to bail out and escape with only a broken ankle.

The super-fast executive airplane Ted Wells was designing was another project he was doing on his own time. He tentatively called it the Model 17 because the most recent airplane the Travel Air Division of Curtiss Wright had been working on had been designated the Model 16.

The Model 17 was to be a brute of a cabin-class biplane. Specified to be powered by a 710-horsepower Wright R-1510 radial engine with a double row of cylin-

The streamlined transition from the engine to the cabin is some of the secret to the Staggerwing's speed. Note the flying wire's anchor embedded in the wing to reduce drag.

A nice period portrait of a D17S Staggerwing. Note the elliptical wings and the gently sloping front windshield. *National Air and Space Museum*

The old Pratt and Whitney eagle, enduring symbol of one of America's most successful radial engine series.

ABOVE LEFT: The Staggerwing was well equipped for instrument flying, especially given the day's standards. It even has an artificial horizon (lower right of the pilot's side of the panel), though the six flight instruments are not laid out according to the convention that has since become standard. Note the throwover control column. *National Air and Space Museum*

LEFT: The Staggerwings exquisite retractable landing gear. At Staggerwing speeds the weight and complexity of the retraction mechanism were worth the effort for the speed gained over the faired-in fixed gear.

ders, it was projected to have a top speed approaching 250 miles per hour. Its wings were uniquely arranged. Contrary to general convention, the top wing was positioned further aft than the bottom wing. This negative stagger was the inspiration for the airplane's popular name—the Staggerwing. The upper and lower wings were connected by two streamlined I struts, a design that Wells first used on his biplane racer. Every turn buckle connection was embedded in the wings. Two massive wheelpants enclosed the wheels. The gear was not retractable into the fuselage, but the wheels could be retracted partially into the wheelpants to reduce drag.

According to Wells, the negative stagger configuration was selected exclusively to maximize the pilot's upward and lateral visibility. It also had structural and weight and balance benefits, however.

Walter Beech was thrilled by Wells' design and proposed the production of the Model 17 to Curtiss Wright. The company felt it was too big a risk in the depressed economic conditions and turned the project down. It was just the response Beech needed. He was an entrepreneur at heart. His personality wasn't suited for a career as just one more salaried executive in a mega-corporation. He decided to leave Curtiss Wright and start

Mega-Staggerwings

Ted Wells' initial specifications for the Model 17 called for a 710-horsepower Wright twin-row radial engine, but the first Staggerwing, the Model 17R, was built with a 420-horsepower Wright because the larger engine wasn't yet certified. As it turned out, the 420-horsepower version delivered astounding performance in its own right, but proved too expensive and the market ultimately demanded a scaled-down, less-powerful version of the Staggerwing, the B17L.

But Beechcraft did go on to build two Staggerwings equipped with monster engines. They were both one-of-a-kind aircraft, the Model A17F with a 690-horsepower Wright Cyclone and the A17FS with a supercharged version of the Cyclone, which boosted power up to 710 horsepower.

The A17F was in all probability not going to be built following the good performance of the 17R, were it not for the age-old American marketing tactic of advertising a product that was barely on the drawing board. Walter Beech proudly advertised in the company sales brochures the availability of the Model 17 in two versions because it looked better to have more than one type in production.

In the meantime he focused his efforts exclusively on finding customers for the 17R, but the ad for the bigger airplane caught the eye of the executives of the Goodall-Worsted Company of Sanford, Maine. In early 1934 the company checked out the specs and without much further ado placed an order for a Model A17F accompanied by an $8,000 deposit check. Since up to that point Beechcraft had built exactly one airplane and had only one other order on the books, Walter Beech wasn't about to admit that the ad was mostly hype. Beechcraft was going to build the A17F.

Like the 17R, the A17F had steel tube main spars and its airframe was similar in most other respects, except for the drag flaps mounted on its upper wings. But its monster engine made it an entirely different animal. It cruised at 205 miles per hour, a higher speed than the maximum speed of the 17R. The greater torque of its bigger engine made it much more of a handful during takeoff and landing than the 17R. In the air, however, it was every bit as much of a delight as its less-powerful sib-

ling, winning high praise from the government test pilot who conducted the DOT tests.

Decked out in Goodall-Worsted colors and upholstered in the finest cloth the company made, the A17F proved to be an outstanding executive transport. It thundered mostly between the company's Sanford, Maine, headquarters and its textile mills in Ohio and Tennessee.

From Goodall-Worsted the big Staggerwing went first to Howard Hughes and then to Harold Smith, a wealthy corporate executive who allowed one of his pilots, Robert Perlick, to fly it in the Bendix Trophy Race of 1937. Smith and Perlick's enthusiasm was no doubt fueled by Louise Thaden's Bendix victory in a smaller stock Staggerwing the previous year, and the success of Benny Howard's big cabin-class *Mr. Mulligan*.

Filled to the gills with 381 gallons of fuel instead of the normal 155 gallons, the A17F lumbered down Burbank's runway at the start of the race, and its landing gear promptly collapsed under its heavy load. Miraculously there was no fire, and Perlick scrambled out of the cockpit window without a scratch.

He was back the next year, now also the owner of the A17F as well as its pilot. The airplane had been strengthened to carry the extra fuel and had a new engine that was goosed all the way up to 745 horsepower. Perlick flew like a demon, averaging 260 miles per hour, and he seemed set to win when close to the end of the race the engine quit. The bitterly disappointed pilot kept his cool and made a successful emergency landing. After being so close to victory he sadly ended up barely a footnote in the Bendix Trophy story instead of a major celebrity.

The other Mega-Staggerwing, the 710-horsepower A17FS with a cruise speed of 225 miles per hour, was built specifically to be flown by Louise Thaden in the 1934 MacRobertson International Trophy Race from Great Britain to Australia. But Thaden's funding didn't come together and she had to withdraw. The fastest, most powerful, and most expensive Staggerwing ever built became a white elephant, briefly used by the Bureau of Air Commerce to transition its pilots into complex airplanes.

The 690-horsepower Beech A17F Staggerwing custom-made for the Goodall Worsted Company of Sanford, Maine.

his own company with his wife, Olive Ann, to build the ultimate executive airplane. They took Ted Wells with them as chief engineer and full-fledged partner.

The Beeches and Wells had been moved to St. Louis by Curtiss Wright, but they returned to Wichita, Kansas, to establish Beechcraft. By May 1932 a small group of highly skilled ex-Travel Air employees was on the Beechcraft payroll, hard at work on the Model 17 in premises rented from the mothballed Cessna Aircraft Company.

Beech and Wells decided to build the first prototype with a 420-horsepower Wright R-975-E2 engine because the more powerful R-1510 hadn't yet been approved by the Department of Commerce. The airplane was officially designated the Model 17R.

The Staggerwing is often referred to as a revolutionary aircraft, and it was one in the sense that it pioneered the concept of a corporate aircraft designed to have the highest performance available for its time. It was a design philosophy that many years later would inspire Bill Lear to create the Learjet.

In its construction, however, the Model 17R was quite conventional. Like most aircraft of the day, it had a steel tube fuselage with nonstructural wooden formers to give it the desired shape. Dural metal panels (dural being an aluminum alloy commonly used in aircraft manufacturing) covered the fuselage through the cabin section, and fabric was used aft of the cabin. The wing had steel tube spars and its spruce wing ribs were densely spaced to maintain the airfoil's integrity. The wing leading edge was covered in dural, and the completed panels were covered in fabric.

The liberal use of fairings achieved an extraordinarily clean airframe. The airplane also had all the systems bells and whistles available, which was noteworthy at a time when having brakes was still considered a luxury in some circles. One novel feature was a split rudder. The left and right sides of the rudder could be displaced outward simultaneously to act as an air brake. It was an innovative design but proved marginally effective in subsequent flight tests and wasn't used on production Staggerwings.

Construction of the prototype progressed rapidly. Wells was also slowly wading through the demanding design review process of the Aeronautics Branch of the Department of Commerce to acquire the airplane's ATC. The relatively inexperienced young engineer found the stress analysis requirements particularly challenging.

On November 5, 1932, the Model 17R, gleaming in the maroon and red colors that would become a signature Beechcraft color combination, was ready for it first flight. With test pilot Wilbur "Pete" Hill at the

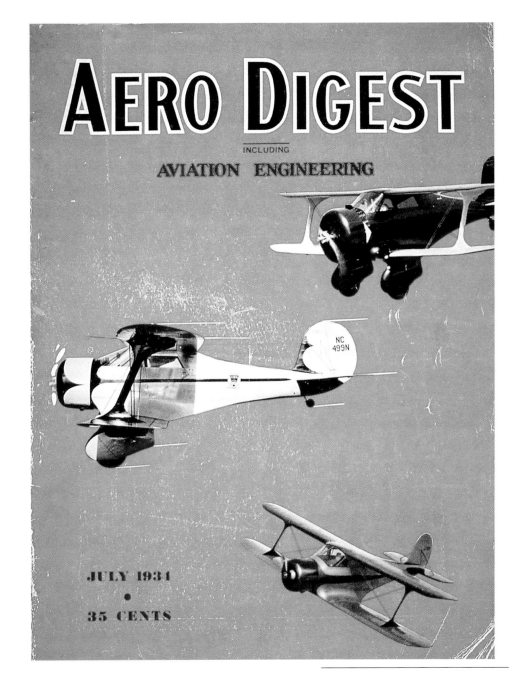

controls, the first Staggerwing thundered into the air for a perfect maiden flight. Hill rapidly opened up the flight envelope in the next few days, and on November 11 the 17R attained an airspeed of 201.2 miles per hour. It was unheard-of performance for a cabin-class personal airplane, in league with the famous Mystery Ship racer just as Walter Beech had promised.

The Model 17R received its ATC on December 20. Beech was free to show it off across the country to drum up sales. The sales tours revealed some empen-

A 1934 *Aero Digest* cover portraying all three Staggerwings made until then. Upper right, a one-of-a-kind A17F, 690-horsepower Staggerwing custom built for the Goodall Worsted Company of Sanford, Maine. Center, the 420-horsepower B17R, the first Staggerwing to fly. Lower right, the 225-horsepower B17L, the first production Staggerwing.

Announcement of the 1932 UIC cabin Waco. Note the improved cowling with speed blisters over the rocker box covers.

Largest Sale of Any Aviation Magazine

POPULAR AVIATION

AUGUST
25c

Waco "C"
See Page 89

THE ARUP FLYING WING

How the Tail Group is Built

LEVITATION — a new system of Flight

The armed forces used the Staggerwing for liaison duties, ordering 412 D17S models, of which 103 served with the Royal Air Force as the Traveller Mark 1. Many of these aircraft were reconverted for civilian use at war's end. *National Air and Space Museum*

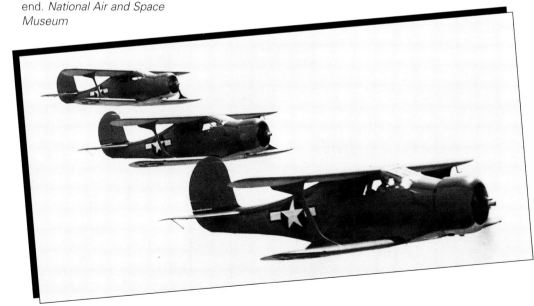

nage vibration that was dampened by a rearrangement of the tail's flying wires after some wrangling with the DOC inspectors.

While the 17R met its design specifications handsomely, it seemed that Beech may have miscalculated what the cream of the business community was willing to pay for high-speed luxury. Potential cus-

tomers were amazed by the airplane's performance on the demo tours during the spring of 1933, but they balked at the $18,000 sticker price. There was only one taker, the Loffland Brothers oil company of Tulsa, Oklahoma. The company had been flying a fleet of five Travel Airs, and its owner, Tom Loffland, was an old friend of Walter Beech. As the launch customer for the Staggerwing he got the 17R at a healthy discount.

The lack of sales convinced Beech and Wells that although you can never be too far ahead of the pack in performance, you could be way ahead in price. They realized that there was plenty of room in the design to simplify the airframe and equip it with a lower powered, lower cost engine and still fly circles around any Stinson or Waco. The Staggerwing "lite" could be offered for around $8,000, not outrageously more than the less capable competition. And later, as the type carved out market share, they could easily ratchet back up the horsepower at any time.

Beechcraft developed and built the simplified Staggerwing during late 1933 and into 1934, calling it the B17L. Its sleek airframe projected great power and grace and established the classic Staggerwing look that would change little over the years. Gone were the massive fixed gears of the 17R, replaced by wheels that retracted into the wings and looked dainty by comparison. Spruce replaced the steel tube spars in the wing, and the airfoil was changed to enhance low speed handling. The split rudder was history, replaced by split flaps on the lower wings. Instead of the hefty gas-guzzling Wright, there was an economic 225-horsepower Jacobs radial up front. A 50-gallon fuel tank was standard with the option to increase fuel capacity to 70 or 90 gallons.

When the B17L took to the air for the first time in the spring of 1934, the results were impressive. Its cruise speed was 162 miles per hour, and it had a range of 600 miles with standard tanks. In comparison the Stinson SR-5 Reliant, which was equipped with the same horsepower, poked along at 120 miles per hour and had a reach of only 390 miles. The Staggerwing cost only $2,000 more. It fascinated the flying community as much as the 17R had, but it also found buyers.

Beech moved the company into his old haunt, the Travel Air factory, to have more space for producing the B17L. He had booked 17 firm orders for the airplane by the time it received its ATC at the end of 1934. The gamble on which he had staked his entire fortune at the depth of the Depression was beginning to pay off. For the first time the company showed a small profit, and as the economy slowly began to regain its momentum the Staggerwing was perfectly positioned to take advantage of it.

When the Staggerwing made its first appearance, it reinforced the keen interest in high-performance cabin-class airplanes of Benjamin "Benny" Howard, the man behind the wildly successful DGA racers. With characteristic flair he chose a novel way to enter the field. He would design a four-seat cabin-class executive airplane that would be fast enough to win the most prestigious air races, competing against the highly specialized aircraft built exclusively for racing. While it wouldn't be as fast as its closest competitors, on cross-country races it would have the time advantage by needing fewer fuel stops and being able to fly higher to avoid weather. With the publicity a string of victories would set off, Howard hoped that orders for the machine would quickly follow.

To help him realize the bold new scheme, Benny Howard was once again joined by Gordon Israel, the talented young engineer who had worked with him on his racer designs. They completed the high-wing cabin monoplane in only four months, in time for the 1934 racing season. It was the DGA-6, but it would come to be universally known by its racing name, *Mister Mulligan*.

Power, speed, and luxury, the Staggerwing offered high performance and impeccable sytle.

A wind-driven generator on a Waco QDC, practically foolproof in its simplicity. The tiny propeller turns a coil inside the generator, which provides electrical power in flight and also charges the battery. The propeller keeps turning in the air stream even in case of engine failure.

The Gull Wing Stinson was the ultimate refinement of the Reliant line. Introduced in 1936 it got its gull wing, which is really a double tapered wing, from the low-wing Stinson Model A airliner. It was optimized for low drag and high lift to get the airliner in and out of the small grass fields of the day, yet allow it good en route speed. In addition to the civilian models, 500 Gull Wing Stinsons were built for the RAF for instrument and navigation trainers. *Jim Koepnick/EAA*

A Stinson SR-9 Gull Wing on a proverbial sunny afternoon. These aircraft were also state of the art transportation in more challenging weather, favored by corporations and regional air charter services in addition to private owners.

Mister Mulligan was a formidable performer. Its clean, light, conventionally constructed airframe had exceptionally low drag, achieved by what Howard and Israel cornily called the "go-grease" treatment. The all-wood wing had a high-speed airfoil, and wooden formers and fairings made the fuselage a teardrop continuation of the tightly cowled engine. The top surface of the fuselage was a flat, narrowing extension of the wing surface to maintain airflow continuity. The fixed landing gear structure was also masterfully faired in.

To propel it to its hoped-for victories, *Mister Mulligan* was powered by a hefty 500-horsepower Wright Wasp, which was souped up to belt out a whopping 830 horsepower. The engine alone cost $5,500, but it was all well worth it. When Benny Howard climbed to 17,000 feet in the airplane and set cruise power at 75 percent, *Mister Mulligan* streaked across the sky at 290 miles per hour.

With high hopes Howard sent off pilots Harold Neumann and George Cassidy in *Mister Mulligan* to Burbank, California, to join the start line of the transcontinental Bendix Trophy race. But *Mister Mulligan* never made it. Somewhere over the Rockies as it was cruising at 21,000 feet to avoid a line of clouds, something went wrong with the oxygen system. Overcome by hypoxia, which sneaks up on its victims unnoticed, Cassidy passed out and Neumann became semiconscious. They didn't have long to live, but then their luck changed. The engine quit. Silently *Mister Mulligan* began to descend into the more oxygen-rich air below.

Neumann was too dysfunctional to troubleshoot the engine problem, but somehow he managed to keep the wings level. *Mister Mulligan* had glided below the ridge line of the Rockies by the time Neumann's mind cleared enough to realize that they had run a fuel tank dry. He switched tanks, restarted the engine, and found a small airport where they could land and find out where the hell they were. On landing, a crosswind gust shoved them into an obstruction at the runway's edge. The impact collapsed the landing gear, totaled the propeller, and put an end to *Mister Mulligan's* 1934 Bendix Trophy performance before it had even begun.

Undeterred, Howard and Israel had the wounded bird trucked to Los Angeles for repairs and were at the controls themselves when *Mister Mulligan* thundered into the air from Burbank Airport in a thick fog at the start of the 1935 Bendix Trophy race. This time the oxygen system worked flawlessly as they cruised into Kansas City for their one refueling stop. Then they were off to Cleveland, Ohio, and the finish line.

Nearing Toledo Howard realized to his horror that ever since they took off from Kansas City, 500 miles behind them, they had been flying with the flaps down. Their official all-in speed over the course (including the time spent refueling) worked out to 220 miles per hour. They held their breath. Roscoe Turner had been hot on their heels. His Weddell Williams racer was faster, but he needed three fuel stops. In the end they beat Turner by 23.5 seconds. For years Howard got a kick out of being able to say that he beat Roscoe Turner with his flaps down.

The Bendix Trophy event was followed by the closed circuit Thompson Trophy race, 10 laps of 15 miles each. *Mister Mulligan* was in the thick of it with Harold Neumann at the controls. Roscoe Turner in his faster Weddell Williams was comfortably roaring toward getting his revenge on *Mister Mulligan* for the narrow Bendix defeat. But with only one lap to go Turner's racer blew a cylinder and had to drop out. The big Howard flashed first across the finish line. *Mister Mulligan* was the only airplane ever to win both the Bendix and Thompson trophies in the same year. Not bad for a design that was essentially a souped-up cabin-class business airplane.

The next year's Bendix Trophy was to bring its own share of cabin-class drama. In 1936 for the first

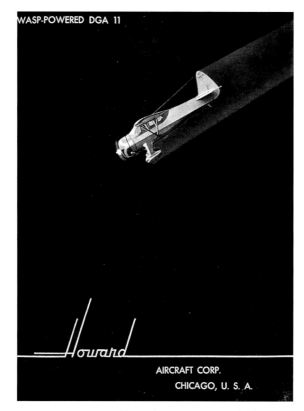

time women were allowed to compete with the men. In addition to the standard prize, a special prize of $2,500 was announced for the first woman to finish. Walter and Olive Ann Beech felt that it would be good publicity to have a stock Staggerwing participate, and they talked Louise Thaden and Blanche Noyes into flying it. Although the Beeches didn't see much of a chance for a first-place finish, they thought the two women would at least have a good shot at the special prize.

For the 1936 model year Beechcraft had upgraded the Staggerwing to the C17 line. Slight adjustments to the landing gear and a realignment of the horizontal stabilizer to counter the earlier model's nose heaviness in the flare were the most significant changes. The airplane was offered with 225-horsepower and 285-horsepower Jacobs engines (the latter being the best seller of the line) and with 285-horsepower and 420-horsepower Wrights.

The top-of-the-line 420-horsepower Wright-powered C17R, with a cruise speed of 202 miles per hour at 10,000 feet, was the one to be flown by Thaden and her copilot, Noyes. The only modification to it was the addition of extra fuel and oil tanks to enable it to fly the 2,700-mile New York–Los Angeles route of the race with one fuel stop in Wichita.

Mister Mulligan, winner of the 1935 Bendix and Thompson trophies. It beat Roscoe Turner's Weddell Williams racer by 23.5 seconds on the Los Angeles–Cleveland route to claim the Bendix, and it won the closed-circuit Thompson when Turner had to drop out because of engine problems. It was the only airplane to win both trophies in the same year. Designed by Benny Howard and Gordon Israel, it was powered by a 500-horsepower Wright Wasp souped up to 830 horsepower. It was the prototype for the Howard DGA cabin class line. *National Air and Space Museum*

Note the emphasis on using the Howard for business flying in this 1939 advertisement. These aircraft could be equipped for instrument flying, being every bit as capable as the airliners of the day. Just about the only condition against which they were defenseless was airframe icing.

OPPOSITE: The Howard DGA was derived from Benny Howard's *Mister Mulligan*. Pictured is a 1939 DGA 11 powered by a 450-horsepower Pratt and Whitney Wasp Jr. It is owned by Gene DeMarco, professional aircraft restorer and chief pilot of the Old Rhinebeck Aerodrome, New York.

The Petroleum Industry is one of the world's largest users of Airplanes.

The 1939 Howard, shown at the right is owned by—MR. GEORGE H. ECHOLS, HOUSTON, TEXAS.

Mr. Echols has large operations in the oil fields of the South.

The 1939 HOWARD is a Business Airplane

Faster and faster goes the tempo of business, and the airplane plays a constantly larger part in the transportation scheme of both "BIG" and "LITTLE" business.

America is a country where individualized transportation has reached the highest mark, yet tomorrow we will witness a "taking to the air" undreamed of yesterday, except by an H. G. Wells, because of the advancements made in the airplanes.

The 1939 Howard 4-5 place cabin airplane powered with proven engines of various horsepower will play an important part in this BUSINESS OF FLYING because it has speeds up to 200 M.P.H. and useful capacity up to 1700 pounds, plus all of the other requisites for safe, comfortable and economical cross-country flight and can be easily converted for many uses. Ask for further information.

Howard AIRCRAFT CORPORATION
5304 WEST 65TH STREET, CHICAGO, ILL., U.S.A.

APRIL 1939

75

Mister Mulligan was back, flown by Howard who was accompanied by his wife. Roscoe Turner was racing again with his 1,000-horsepower Weddell-Williams. Amelia Earhart was entered with Helen Richey in a Lockheed Electra. Joe Jacobson was flying a sleek Northrop Gamma. There was even a DC-2 and the diminutive Laura Ingalls was competing in a big, jet black Lockheed Orion. It was going to be tough for a stock Staggerwing to place in the money against such a field.

Louise Thaden's strategy was to fly the Staggerwing as if she were a typical Beechcraft customer on an everyday long cross-country flight. She knew from experience that endurance flights often ended up resembling the fable of the tortoise and the hare, as tempestuous top-of-the-line racers pushed ruthlessly to their limits fell victim to mechanical glitches far ahead of the pack but short of the finish line. She ran the engine at 65 percent cruise power and, apart from having to dead reckon above bad weather because their Lear ADF radio gave up the ghost, the trip was routine. When they landed in Wichita to refuel and Walter Beech heard they were ambling along in economy cruise, he had a fit, but Thaden ignored him.

The blue Staggerwing with the big white 66 on its side made steady progress toward the L.A. basin. Well within the 6:00 P.M. arrival deadline the two women were peering into the hazy afternoon sun trying to find the airport. Suddenly there it was, right on target. They buzzed the finish line, relieved to have the long day behind them, and touched down over 14 hours after they left New York.

As they taxied in, Thaden and Noyes thought something must be seriously wrong with their airplane. It was swarmed by the crowd waving them frantically out of the Staggerwing. It was only after they opened the cabin door that they realized they had won. Thaden's strategy, a quick turnaround in Wichita, and some bad luck for their competitors had clinched the Bendix Trophy for them. Forty-five minutes later Laura Ingalls touched down in her Orion to claim second place. It was quite a day for women in aviation—and for the Staggerwing.

Over the next few hours the news began to trickle in about what had happened to some of the field's top contenders. *Mister Mulligan* had been doing well all the way into New Mexico, where it lost a propeller blade. Benny Howard and his wife were lucky to survive the ensuing controlled crash, although they were badly injured. Earhart's Electra was slowed way down by a hatch that had popped open (one wonders why they didn't land somewhere and close it). Jacobson parachuted out of his Northrop Gamma, and Turner

The Spartan Executive shown above at Long Beach airport in Los Angeles, California, in the late 1930s.

The Spartan Executive was a far cry from Spartan's first airplane, the C-3 open-cockpit biplane. It was inspired by aircraft like the DC-2 and the sleek all-metal Lockheed Electra. Bill Skelly of Skelly Oil, who owned Spartan, reasoned that oil company executives were ready for a modern personal airliner and would be willing to pay the $23,000 price. Most customers were indeed the oil companies for the 34 Executives built. The airplane pictured is one of seven still flying. It was at Pearl Harbor on December 7, 1941.

was sidelined by mechanical problems. Luck was with Thaden and Noyes in 1936, but that, as they say, makes horse racing.

The Bendix victory was a tremendous publicity coup not only for the Staggerwing but also for personal aviation. It was a dramatic demonstration of the capabilities and the reliability of the personal airplane used for business or pleasure. And the Staggerwing was a far cry from the open-cockpit Travel Air in which Beech had clinched the Ford Reliability Tour a decade before.

By the mid-1930s the large cabin-class airplane was firmly entrenched in the market for personal-business aircraft. Spurred in part by the Staggerwing's luxurious style and high performance, Stinson and Waco both refined their own designs substantially and the three manufacturers dominated the high end of the market.

Stinson's next significant step in developing the Reliant was the SR-7, which was essentially an SR-6 with a new wing. Introduced in 1936, it became commonly known as the Gull Wing Stinson. Bob Ayer had designed an elegant double-tapered monospar wing for

the Stinson's Model A airliner. It was optimized for low drag and high lift to enable the eight-passenger low-wing trimotor to easily slip in and out of the short fields on its commuter hops yet make good time en route.

The Model A's wing proved highly effective and was adapted to replace the straight wing of the SR-6 Reliant. The double-tapered wing was thickest at the strut attach point. This structure gave it a gull-winged appearance, but it wasn't, in fact, truly a gull wing in the manner of the Minimoa glider or the Junkers Ju-87 Stuka dive bomber. Its structure was also a departure from the day's norm for personal aircraft. It contained no wood. Its steel and dural skeleton was covered with dural sheets and fabric.

The wing gave the SR-7 a distinctive, elegant look that anyone considering a Staggerwing had to take seriously as a potential alternative. The SR-7 was offered with 225-, 245-, and 260-horsepower Lycomings. With the latter engine it had a respectable cruise speed of 140 miles per hour and a range of up to 650 miles.

The certification of the Gull Wing Stinson wasn't without its share of excitement. The prototype would-

n't recover from its first spin test, and the test pilots had to bail out. Stall strips solved the problem to the satisfaction of certification criteria, but after the third rotation (six rotations were required by the certification tests) the spin still tended to go flat and the tail vibrated at the edge of acceptability. A subsequent model, the SR-9, had a problem with the wing-strut attachment that resulted in two fatal crashes but proved easy to fix and did no harm to the airplane's reputation in the long term.

Waco solidified its position in the cabin-class market in 1935 by dividing its line into Standard and Custom models. The Standard line was a continuation of the 1934 cabin-class Waco in a stripped-down version at a rock bottom price aimed at cornering the budget market (the YKC of 1934 and YKC-S of 1935 had the same ATC).

The Custom Waco retained some common elements with the Standard model but was a different airplane. It had a scaled-down lower wing, graceful elliptical wingtips, a roomier fuselage, a more rakish, angular vertical stabilizer instead of the rounded homey looking one, and more stylish windows. Many systems features that were extra on the Standard airplanes were included in the base price of the Custom Waco. Its luxuriously appointed cabin held its own with the plushest interiors offered by Stinson and Beechcraft. The Custom Waco came with three engine options, a 210 Continental (not a particularly popular choice) and 225- and 285-horsepower Jacobs engines.

From about 1935 on it is fair to say of all three major manufacturers of large cabin-class airplanes that the changes in their line-up from year to year were largely incremental (except for the Waco E Model of 1939). The basic airframes changed little, and all three companies provided a variety of powerplants for their various models, ranging from 210 to 225 horsepower all the way up to 450 horsepower, and running the gamut of all the engine manufacturers.

Landing gear structures were enhanced, engine cowls were streamlined, and constant speed propellers had become standard. Flaps became increasingly common, ailerons were metalized for certain models, and mass-balanced controls had become the norm.

A good look at the frontal area of a Gull Wing Stinson showing the low-drag profile, except for the radial engine which has to overcome its own drag by brute power.

The Howard DGA's sophisticated cockpit was suitable for instrument flying. It was also a work of art. Flight instruments and engine instruments are clustered on the central panel. The aircraft has a vacuum system to power the gyros.

Howard DGA cockpit, period photo. Note the absence of an artificial horizon in the photo. They were available, but not yet considered mandatory. *National Air and Space Museum*

Incessant tinkering went on with superficial styling and cabin amenities as the airplane makers wholeheartedly embraced the odious "New Model Year" game, a concept they borrowed from the automobile industry.

In 1938 Waco built a version of its Custom model on tricycle gear. It was an ungainly creature and found few takers in a flying community that still referred to the tail wheel configuration as conventional.

Much more impressive was Waco's last and most gorgeous model, the E series, introduced in 1939. It had a beautifully streamlined, thin fuselage with a seamlessly blended engine cowling, and its lower wing was more like a "mini-wing." The wings were first covered in plastic-bonded plywood followed by fabric. Its electric flaps were particularly noteworthy among its advanced features. This Waco was built for speed. The smallest engine for the E model was a 300-horsepower Jacobs on the ARE, but the most popular version was the more powerful SRE with a 450-horsepower Pratt and Whitney Wasp Jr. The SRE cruised at 195 miles per hour at 9,600 feet and had a range of 1,000 miles. Pilots accustomed to earlier Cabin Wacos liked to say the SRE had

Home, James

If you were a British diplomat and didn't fancy a long boat ride home from the New World, an excellent alternative in the mid-1930s was flying home in your own Beech Staggerwing. That, at least, was the opinion of Captain Harold Farquhar (ex-Coldstream Guards) on His Majesty's Service at the British Legation in Mexico City. Farquhar owned the first B17R Staggerwing, the first one powered by a 420-horsepower Wright engine. In 1935 he was due for leave in England and decided, like Columbus and Magellan, to take the scenic route by going west to reach his destination to the east.

Farquhar was accompanied by Fritz Beiler, a German pilot living in Mexico City. The pair first flew up to New York City to get a pair of floats installed. Then they were off through Canada and Alaska, into Siberia, and down to Manchuria, where an officer with the Japanese occupying forces proved very helpful in removing the Staggerwing's floats.

Continuing on in land-plane configuration, they winged their way down to Hong Kong, on to Vietnam, across the rest of Southeast Asia into India, across Iran, Iraq, and the Holy Land, into Egypt, along the North African coast, up into Europe, and across France to England. It took them 152 hours of flying at an average speed of 138 miles per hour, not bad considering that for almost half of the trip they were burdened by floats.

Apart from the usual tricks with the weather, the dubious (but cheap) Soviet gas, and a provincial British colonial bureaucracy that drove Farquhar to distraction, they encountered few difficulties. Like the pilots of the Stearman C-3 the *Flying Carpet*, they weren't in pursuit of records and fame but a personal trip of a lifetime. Flying in much greater luxury than the *Flying Carpet's* pilots, they experienced firsthand how dramatically the capabilities of personal aircraft had increased since Sergeant Beech worked on Jennies at Rich Field only 15 years before.

a "built-in tailwind." Waco was proud enough of it to call it the Aristocrat. Bill Lear was among the lucky few to own one of the 21 Aristocrats built before World War II intervened.

Two other large cabin-class airplanes made their debut in the second half of the 1930s, the cabin Howard DGA and the Spartan Executive. While produced in much smaller numbers than the Stinson Reliants, Cabin Wacos, and Staggerwings, they were nevertheless eminently entitled to claim their share of the limelight.

Ben Howard's scheme to win the hearts and wallets of the captains of industry by winning the Bendix and Thompson Trophies with *Mister Mulligan*, the prototype for his entry into the cabin-class field, paid off. There was strong interest in a commercialized version of the airplane when he established the Howard

Aircraft Company in 1936 in Chicago in premises formerly occupied by Laird.

The prototype for the production version of *Mister Mulligan* was designated the DGA-7 (dubbed *Mister Flanigan*). This airplane had a 420-horsepower Wright engine and essentially *Mister Mulligan's* airframe with a wider wingspan. Only one DGA-7 was built and was used to refine the first production version, the DGA-8. The DGA-8 had a larger vertical stabilizer and was equipped with a 320-horsepower Wright radial, which gave it excellent speed at lower production and operating costs than the bigger engine. The DGA-8 could cruise at speeds as high as 191 miles per hour at 12,000 feet and had a range of approximately 900 miles.

The DGA-8's airframe was of conventional mixed construction characteristic of the era. The fuselage was steel tube covered with dural metal sheets and fabric. The

A good view of the Staggerwing's extended gear. It looks more fragile than it is but kept Staggerwing pilots on their toes. *Jim Koepnick/EAA*

97

wing skeleton was made of spruce and plywood. It was covered with a plywood sheet, which in turn was covered by fabric. This technique produced a wing that was particularly light, strong, and torsion resistant. Other features of the airframe were trailing edge flaps, semicantilevered landing gear, and wheelpants covering both the main wheels and the tail wheel.

With its racing heritage the DGA-8 appealed especially to celebrities. Actor Wallace Beery, an enthusiastic pilot who owned several aircraft, was an early customer.

The cabin DGA was basically a custom-built airplane, and it wasn't long before other engine options became available. The Model 9 and 12 had 285- and 300-horsepower Jacobs engines, respectively. The Model 11, which was certified in 1938, came with the hefty 450-horsepower Pratt and Whitney Wasp Jr. and had slightly more wing area and a roomier fuselage. Even at 65 percent power it could cruise at 203 miles per hour at 10,000 feet and had a reach of more than 1,000 miles. It is considered by many Howard enthusiasts to be the best of the cabin DGAs. A worthy contemporary of the Staggerwing, it offered an excellent alternative for pilots who preferred a monoplane.

The cabin DGAs had exquisite, richly upholstered art deco cabins. Elegantly streamlined housings for each of the control columns protruded from the spacious, elliptic, wood-veneered instrument panel, creating a faintly marine atmosphere. More than 70 cabin Howard DGAs were produced for the civilian market by the time Pearl Harbor was attacked and America went to war.

The ultimate art deco cabin-class airplane was the Spartan Executive. A modern all-metal low-wing monoplane with retractable gear, it had more in common with the DC-3 airliner than with its cabin-class contemporaries. Next to the Spartan Executive, Staggerwings, Cabin Wacos, Reliants, and even the Howards looked quaintly dated. And the big Spartan had the performance to match its futuristic looks.

The concept of the Spartan Executive originated in 1934. As the economy was slowly recovering, so were the fortunes of Skelly Oil, owner of the mothballed Spartan Aircraft Company. Bill Skelly and Spartan's manager, Ed Hudlow, took a look at the sleek, modern, all-metal commercial airplanes like the DC-2 and the Lockheed Electra and reasoned that a small niche of forward thinking entrepreneurial executives would prefer a personal business airplane designed along similar lines. Yet their choice was limited to aircraft which, though capable enough, were increasingly beginning to look like the creations of a time that was slowly receding.

Skelly and Hudlow hired the highly experienced designer, James Ford, to turn their idea into reality. The airplane's design and development was considered a small-scale custom project and proceeded in virtual secrecy. By early 1936 the prototype was approaching its first flight, and it looked like no other cabin-class airplane. It was more like a cross between the day's most modern fighter and airliner. It was called the Standard Seven and was powered by a 285-horsepower Jacobs engine. Its only odd feature was a long dorsal fin, which blended into a small vertical stabilizer that looked rather inadequate.

The Spartan's first flight took place in March 1937 in the hands of famed test pilot Eddie Allen who was imported to Tulsa especially for the occasion. The first flights, while promising, proved the airplane to be underpowered and the vertical stabilizer to be, indeed, inadequate.

The redesigned model took shape by the end of the year, equipped with a 400- to 450-horsepower Pratt and Whitney Wasp Jr., a conventional vertical stabilizer, and a more streamlined cowling. The big Pratt and Whitney certainly cured the power shortage

The artificial horizon and the directional gyro were the tools that made instrument flight possible, and vastly expanded the utility and reliability of the airplane.

The breather holes for the supercharger of the 450-horsepower Pratt and Whitney Wasp Jr., the engine of choice of the super cabin class.

Propeller technology progressed rapidly from 1920 to 1936. Initially the metal propeller was one piece of forged aluminum. Then came the ground adjustable propeller, which could be set prior to take-off for climb or cruise pitch depending on the purpose of the flight. The final stage was the controllable pitch propeller that allowed for adjustments in flight and is still with us today.

that had plagued the prototype. The revised version cruised at 210 miles per hour at 75 percent power and had a reach of 850 miles. It received its certification in February 1937 and went into production as the Model 7-W. To link it in the minds of the public to its target market, it was named the Spartan Executive.

The Spartan Executive's construction appeared to be on the leading edge of the day's airframe technology but had some characteristics under its metal skin that originated from the past it had vowed to leave behind. The fuselage structure, though suggestive in appearance of monocoque construction, was a steel tube frame, which carried dural bulkheads and stringers and was skinned with dural sheet.

The cantilever monospar wing was built around a welded triangular steel tube spar and had all-metal truss-type wing ribs. The whole assembly was skinned with dural sheet. The center section of the wings was an integral part of the fuselage structure to which the stubby outer wing panels were attached. The ailerons were all-metal skeletons covered with fabric. The electrically operated split flaps were mounted in three sections along the trailing edge of the wing's inner sections and across the belly of the

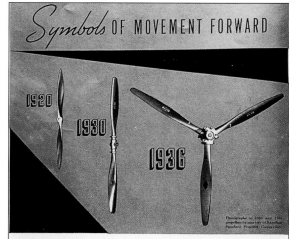

Performance Comparison, Cabin Wacos

The evolution of the Cabin Waco from the first model introduced in 1931 to the last one brought out in 1940 reveals an impressive increase in capabilities in less than a decade.

	Waco QDC	Waco YKC	Waco SRE
	1931	1935	1940
Engine	Continental	Jacobs	Pratt & Whitney Wasp Jr.
	165 hp	225 hp	250 hp
Seats	4	4	4/5
Max. speed (mph)	116	149	202
Cruise speed (mph)	102	130	195
Range (stat. miles)	400	480	1,070
Gross weight (lb)	2,581	3,000	4,200
Useful load (lb)	977	1,050	1,466
Price	$5,985	$6,450	$18,900

fuselage. The landing gear had a wide wheelbase and retracted inward, but the retracted tires rested in the wheel wells uncovered.

As Skelly had foreseen, the majority of customers for the airplane were oil companies. Standard Oil, Texaco, Halliburton, Condor Petroleum Company, Roberts Drilling Company, Wynn Crosby Drilling Company, Lee Drilling Company, and the Bodine Drilling Company all flew Spartans. They were the type of buyer who could afford its shocking $23,000 sticker price. It occasioned not a little envy and jealousy on the part of those who could afford "only" a Staggerwing.

One customer who had no difficulty affording the Spartan was King Ghazi of Iraq. *The Eagle of Iraq* was upholstered in the royal colors, the crown was prominently displayed inside and outside the airplane, and the tail was adorned with the royal coat of arms. But the glittering Spartan wasn't to treat the King to a bird's-eye view of his beloved Baghdad for long. When World War II broke out, Britain's Royal Air Force laid claim to *The Eagle of Iraq* and promptly totaled it in a blown landing somewhere in Scotland.

The Spartan was expensive because it was tremendously labor intensive to produce and also because

Skelly didn't see any potential for large-scale mass production, which precluded the option of keeping unit prices down in anticipation of volume sales. Only 34 Spartan Executives were made. Approximately a third of the fleet is still flying, and the survivors are among the most treasured antiques today.

The large cabin-class airplanes reigned supreme over the world of personal and business flying by the end of the 1930s, but their days as mainstream production machines were numbered. What would eventually lead to their demise was the appearance of an alternative to their behemoth, gas-guzzling radial engines.

At the very end of the 1930s the small, light, horizontally opposed "flat-four" engine gained a foothold in the personal airplane industry. At first the power output of these engines was modest, around 40 to 50 horsepower, but they were embraced enthusiastically by

The Spartan emblem lives on.

New for 1938 in Waco's cabin line-up was the awkward-looking tricycle gear cabin Waco. It joined the standard and custom Wacos but had limited success.

FAR RIGHT: The Waco SRE was the ultimate cabin Waco, on par with anything Beech had to offer. In 1940 it came too late to make much of an impact, but was highly regarded. This aircraft is owned by former astronaut Frank Borman, commander of the first Apollo spacecraft to circle the moon. *Jim Koepnick/EAA*

Bill Lear posing with his Waco SRE. He frequently changed aircraft to publicize his Learadio avionics business. At some point or other he appears to have owned cabin-class aircraft from most manufacturers. He later joined forces with Gordon Israel, who helped Benny Howard design the Howard DGA, to develop the Learjet.

the aircraft manufacturers. In less than a decade they were putting out as much as 300 horsepower at a fraction of the production and operating cost of the big radials. Their small size and light weight allowed aircraft manufacturers to produce lighter, smaller, and less-expensive airframes to match and achieve the same range of performance offered by radial-engined aircraft at a fraction of the costs. In the aftermath of World War II these efficient new designs were soon produced by the thousands, and the big, beautiful, lovingly hand-crafted cabin-class airplanes were priced out of production.

Paradoxically, World War II, which is sometimes seen as having been the death knell for the large cabin-class era, gave several of these aircraft types a tremendous last hurrah that led to their production in numbers, which approached, and in some cases far exceeded, their production levels in peacetime.

In the early days of World War II there was an urgent need for liaison and training aircraft both in Britain and the United States. Many civilian aircraft were appropriated for these roles on an emergency

A good view of the Staggerwing's curvaceous fuselage. The pattern of formers is discernible under the fabric.

The Spartan Executive had metal split flaps in three sections, including a belly flap.

If this picture was black and white, it would be impossible to tell that it was taken today rather than the 1930s. A Spartan Excecutive and a Howard DGA (front) await another flight half a century after they first took to the air.

Performance Comparison, Large Cabin Class

By the end of the 1930s the large cabin-class aircraft reigned supreme among personal-business aircraft. Their performance represented an astonishing increase in less than 20 years over the Curtiss Jenny, which was just about the only personal airplane available in America when the people who created the large cabin class began their careers in aviation.

	Curtiss	Stinson	Beech
	JN-4D	Reliant SR-10F	Staggerwing D17S
	1917	1938	1937
Engine	OX-5	Pratt & Whitney Wasp Jr.	Pratt & Whitney Wasp Jr.
	90 hp	450 hp	450 hp
Seats	2	4/5	4/5
Max. speed (mph)	75	195	212
Cruise speed (mph)	65	177	202
Range (stat. miles)	160	850	800
Gross weight (lb)	1,920	4,650	4,250
Useful load (lb)	490	1,605	1,660
Price	$3,500	$18,000	$18,870
(1924 surplus $500)			

	Howard	Spartan	Waco
	DGA 11	Executive	SRE
	1938	1938	1940
Engine	Pratt & Whitney Wasp Jr.	Pratt & Whitney Wasp Jr.	Pratt & Whitney Wasp Jr.
	450 hp	450 hp	450 hp
Seats	4/5	4/5	4/5
Max. speed (mph)	210	212	202
Cruise speed (mph)	203	208	195
Range (stat. miles)	1,040	850	1,070
Gross weight (lb)	4,100	4,400	4,200
Useful load (lb)	1,650	1,413	1,466
Price	$17,685	$23,500	$18,900

FAR LEFT: Only the basics, but they still get the cabin Waco anywhere its owner wants to go.

View from a Stinson Detroiter as it might have looked in 1934 with TWA's state-of-the-art DC-2 on its takeoff roll.

basis, but the armed forces were also urgently placing orders for new aircraft. The large cabin-class airplanes were perfect for liaison duty and could also serve as advanced trainers for instrument flying and navigation. Their makers eagerly sought their share of the lucrative production contracts put out by the armed forces, and some were not disappointed.

Beechcraft received 412 orders for the 450-horsepower Pratt and Whitney–powered D17S Staggerwing. In peacetime the company made only 68 of them. The model was designated the UC-43 by the Army Air Corps and the GB-2 by the Navy. The Staggerwings served almost exclusively as VIP transports throughout the world. Many of them were seconded to allied nations under the Lend Lease program. Britain's Royal Air Force and Royal Navy received 105 Staggerwings, which they called the Traveller Mk. 1.

Stinson initially shut down the Reliant production line, but in 1942 it got a contract to make 500 Reliants

There is nothing like waking up a 450-horsepower Pratt and Whitney at the crack of dawn with the promise of a long flying day ahead.

In spite of its modern looks, the Spartan relied on some old-fashioned construction techniques. Its fuselage was not of monocoque construction but a steel tube cage to which metal formers are attached that carry the nonstructural metal skin. Its powerplant was the 450-horsepower Pratt and Whitney Wasp Jr. that had become standard for the top cabin biplanes.

OPPOSITE: Beech Staggerwing off the California coast. Note the mass balance on the elevator. Mass balancing of the control surfaces became critical to avoid flutter once aircraft started pushing beyond 150 miles per hour. *Richard Vander Meulen*

for the Royal Navy under the Lend Lease program. They were designated the V-77 by the factory (by then Stinson was being managed by Vultee in the Consolidated-Vultee empire) and served as navigational trainers. Their military designation was AT-19. Most of the AT-19s were used in the United States where large groups of British pilots came for training.

Howard hit the jackpot with a U.S. Navy order for 663 DGA-15s, powered by 450-horsepower Pratt and Whitneys. The Navy used 458 of them as light transports and the rest as instrument trainers.

Waco and Spartan didn't receive contracts to mass produce their cabin-class airplanes for military use, but were soon contributing in other ways. Waco made 600 military trainer versions of its UPF-7 open-cockpit biplanes and designed the ultimate cabin-class glider, the CG-4 troop carrier that would gain fame over the beaches of Sicily and Normandy and along the Rhine. Waco, Beechcraft, and Cessna joined forces in Wichita to mass produce the CG-4.

Spartan contributed by converting the Spartan School of Aeronautics into a major training center for

Note the brass fuel line running from the wing tank into the engine of the cabin Waco QDC.

The Gullwing Stinson served American Airlines' feeder routes in addition to being a popular private and business airplane. American Airlines was formed in the 1930s from several regional lines.

pilots and mechanics. The company also made a primary training biplane for the Navy, the NP-1. While fulfillment of the Navy's order for 200 of these trainers didn't go smoothly because of Spartan's lack of experience with mass production, the airplane did take hundreds of Navy pilots on their first solo flight, among them George Herbert Walker Bush, who would later become the 41st president of the United States. Spartan, which was personally run during the war by millionaire oil man J. Paul Getty, who had bought the Skelly Oil Company and its holdings, also produced B-24 parts. And most civilian Spartan Executives were pressed into service, to the great delight of the brass that got them as VIP transports.

When the war was over, so was the heyday of the large cabin-class biplanes and monoplanes. The military Staggerwings, Reliants, Howards, and others that served so well rejoined their civilian brethren. Supported by a seemingly inexhaustible supply of war surplus radial engines, they gracefully winged their way into the world of cherished antiques in the coming years. Over half a century later they thrill us still, as their thundering radials take us back into a golden age most of us never knew.

SPORTSMEN PILOTS

While the large cabin-class airplanes held the spotlight at the high end of personal and corporate aviation and were largely flown for business, often by professional pilots, the 1930s also saw a remarkable blossoming of sport aviation. Fairchild, a resurrected Cessna, Monocoupe, Luscombe, Rearwin, a new Ryan, and others produced a vast selection of smaller, mostly cabin-class aircraft in the 70- to 145-horsepower range, which were flown primarily by their well-to-do owners and mostly for the sheer fun of it.

Many of these "sportsmen" pilots, as they were then called (although there were also quite a few women among them), thought nothing of hopping into their exotic machines in, say, Chicago, and dashing off to Miami or New York, or Mexico City. Most stayed closer to home, slipping away into the sky merely to be awed by the wondrous new experience of flight. One of the most respected aviation magazines of the day, famous for its flight test reports, was the *Sportsman Pilot.* There was even a Sportsman Pilot's Association, and not a few of its members relished the thought of having some bond by association with such aviation heroes (for

The Monocoupe 110 was the quintessential Sportsman pilot's airplane. Powered by a 110-horsepower Warner Scarab, it represented the maturing of the Monocoupe line. It was a favorite of racing pilots like Johnny Livingston, who highly modified them and cleaned up in the speed events, especially in clipped-wing Monocoupes. *Jim Koepnick/EAA*

National Air and Space Museum

that's what they were in a way we no longer understand) as Jimmy Doolittle, Roscoe Turner, Amelia Earhart, and the Lone Eagle himself, Charles Lindbergh.

Most of the airplanes they flew were technologically conservative, but one or two manufacturers were beginning to adapt the most modern concepts of commercial aircraft design and production. Their experi-

The Monocoupe 110 was the outgrowth of the Monocoupe 90, pictured in this Mono-Aircraft product line-up. The Monocoupe 90 and the 90-A with the NACA cowl were the most popular Monocoupes.

The Fairchild 24, introduced in 1931, was a small two-seat cabin monoplane with a 90-horsepower inline Cirrus engine. It changed markedly over the years, growing into a 175-horsepower four-seater, but never quite as big as the large cabin-class airplanes. It was well liked by recreational pilots because of its excellent handling characteristics and economic operating costs. A late-model F-24 on short final.

Fairchild 24 ready for departure in the late 1930s. *National Air and Space Museum*

ence would contribute, along with the small horizontally opposed four-cylinder engine that would launch Piper, Taylorcraft, and Aeronca on their own golden age, to redefining the world of personal aviation following World War II.

One of the more remarkable developments in the light aircraft industry during the mid-1930s was the resurrection of the Cessna Aircraft Company by Clyde Cessna's nephews, the Wallace brothers, who would create the Airmaster, one of the most exquisite and capable personal airplanes of the time. Dwane Wallace loved his uncle's airplanes and in spite of the company's collapse in the stock-market crash, he became an aeronautical engineer and earned his pilot's license in a Travel Air.

In 1933, with his diploma in hand, he found employment at, of all places, the fledgling Beechcraft Corporation operating in Cessna's closed facilities. Walter Beech put him to work on the big A17F that was being custom built for the Goodall-Worsted Company of Sanford, Maine.

As Wallace began his career at Beechcraft it was already becoming apparent that the personal aircraft market may be recovering. He was becoming increas-

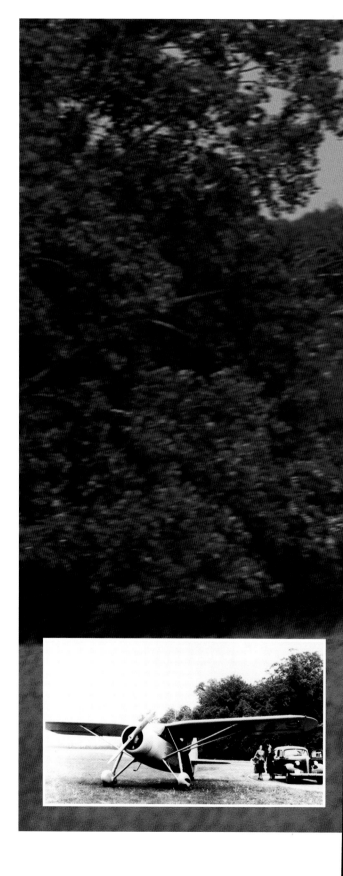

The Fairchild 24 line-up in 1938. The company continued to produce inline Ranger-equipped Fairchilds even after starting to offer radial-engined versions.

An inline Ranger-powered Fairchild 24 passing over the Golden Gate bridge. San Francisco and Oakland are in the background. Pan American's flying boats left from the bay for the Far East during this period. *National Air and Space Museum*

ingly convinced that the time might be ripe for reopening Cessna. The company would need to bring out a modern airplane if it was to re-enter the market, and Wallace had just the right one on his personal drawing board. It was based on the Cessna Model A and was aimed at a market niche above the Fairchilds and the Monocoupes and below the entry-level models of the large cabin class.

A bigger problem than having a new airplane design was convincing Cessna's shareholders to reopen the company. To overcome this obstacle Dwane Wallace enlisted the help of his brother, Dwight, who was an attorney. The two siblings mounted an intensive campaign to win shareholders over to their cause and worked hard at acquiring the stock of the holdouts. Their efforts paid off, and in January 1934 the Cessna Aircraft Company was back in business with Clyde Cessna as president and the Wallace brothers at the helm. Clyde Cessna's position was largely a ceremonial assignment that he agreed to accept to provide some management continuity in the eyes of the market until his untried nephews got the company back on its feet.

The development of the new Cessna, to be called the C-34, could begin in earnest. Fortuitously

THE NEW CESSNA AIRMASTER
The World's
Most Efficient Airplane

CESSNA AIRCRAFT COMPANY • WICHITA. KANSAS • U.S.A.
EXPORT AGENT • AVIATION EQUIPMENT & EXPORT, INC.
CABLE ADDRESS "AVIQUIPO" • 25 BEAVER ST., NEW YORK, N. Y.

The Cessna Airmaster. Clyde Cessna's nephews, Dwane and Dwight Wallace, put their uncle's factory back in business as the Depression began to loosen its grip. They developed the C-34 from the Cessna A series, using the same cantilever-wing concept. Equipped with a 145-horsepower Warner Super Scarab engine, it won the *Detroit News* Trophy efficiency race twice in a row and was officially declared the world's most efficient airplane. The C-37 above is the 1937 model year of the series. Left is the C-38.

Performance Comparison, Sport Aircraft

Pilots electing to fly primarily for fun had many choices by the second half of the 1930s. To get a flavor of the options available and the respective performance figures and costs, it is interesting to compare the open-cockpit Ryan ST-A, the cabin Monocoupe 90-A, and one of the first metal light aircraft with a small horizontally opposed flat-four engine, the Luscombe 8.

	Ryan ST-A 1935	Monocoupe 90-A 1936	Luscombe 8 1938
Engine	Mescano 125 hp	Lambert 90 hp	Continental 65 hp
Seats	2	2	2
Max. speed (mph)	150	130	115
Cruise speed (mph)	127	112	102
Range (stat. miles)	350	525	370
Gross weight (lb)	1,570	1,610	1,200
Useful load (lb)	543	643	535
Price	$4,685	$3,485	$1,975

Beechcraft needed more space to ramp up production of the B17L and moved to the old Travel Air plant, returning the factory to Cessna.

At the core of the C-34 was a cantilevered wing based on the trademark wing of the Cessna Model A, but with a more advanced higher lift airfoil and trailing edge flaps. The wing structure was spruce and plywood with steel-stiffening straps between the double spars to reinforce torsional rigidity. Plywood covered the leading edge, and the entire surface was covered with fabric.

The fuselage was welded steel tube. It was much roomier than the Cessna Model A and better insulated. Notable features were the cantilevered landing gear and the NACA cowling on the nose. The engine chosen for the C-34 was the 145-horsepower Warner Super Scarab engine with a fixed-pitch propeller, a step up from the Model A's 110-horsepower Scarab.

The C-34 was flown for the first time on August 10, 1934, by George Harte, and subsequent speed trials confirmed that the company had an economic speed merchant on its hands. On only 145 horsepower it reg-istered a top speed of 162 miles per hour, it cruised at a blistering 143 miles per hour, and it had a range of 550 miles burning only about 8 gallons of fuel per hour.

In June 1935 the C-34 received its airworthiness certificate. It generated a slow but steady stream of orders immediately and soon production was running at three airplanes per month, a good start under the economic circumstances. Priced at $4,985 it exceeded the performance of many similarly priced larger aircraft with more powerful engines that were much more expensive to operate.

Given the C-34's hot performance, Dwane Wallace and his colleagues were eager to take it on the air-racing circuit. They were particularly keen to enter the *Detroit News* Trophy Race, the circuit's most prestigious efficiency event, held annually at the National Air Races. It rated an airplane's efficiency based on a formula that took into account speed, operating economy, minimum takeoff and landing performance, and passenger comfort. It included a 200-mile cross-country race, a closed-circuit speed event, and takeoff and landing trials.

Cessna's Model AW won the *Detroit News* Trophy in 1931. The C-34 won it easily in 1935, and the next year it repeated its performance. Cessna, having won the trophy three times, got to keep it permanently according to the custom of the time, and the C-34 was officially declared the "World's Most Efficient Airplane."

In 1936 the new Cessna Aircraft Company reached another milestone. Clyde Cessna became convinced that the company he founded was solidly back in business and decided to retire, officially handing over the reins to Dwane Wallace.

For the 1937 model year a widened cabin and some minor enhancements turned the C-34 into the C-37. The following year more substantial changes appeared on the next model, the C-38. The trailing edge flaps were replaced by a barn door-like spoiler that extended from the belly. The empennage was slightly enlarged and new, bow-legged landing gear struts widened the wheelbase by about a foot. This model was called the Airmaster, a name that came into common usage for the entire line.

In 1939 the spoilers were gone, the flaps were back on the wings where they belonged, and Cessna added the 165-horsepower Warner Scarab as an alternative choice to the original 145-horsepower engine. To make it easy to distinguish the two models, they were designated the C-145 and C-165, depending on the engine installed. The more powerful engine added less than 10 miles per hour to the earlier model's cruise speed, hardly worth the engineering effort.

The fact is that most of the changes to the C series accomplished little and were driven primarily by the need to come out with something "new" from year to year. Cessna had gotten the original C-34 so right that little could be done to improve it.

While Dwane Wallace was completing his aeronautical engineering degree and dreaming about rejuvenating his Uncle Clyde's company, Mono-Aircraft corporation, the manufacturer that had cornered the light cabin monoplane market by 1929, was in a bind. By the end of 1930 the company was heavily in debt and was sitting on an inventory of about 25 airplanes, which weren't selling in spite of the overwhelming number of victories its racing Monocoupes had reaped in their class that year.

A day before New Year's Eve Mono-Aircraft Inc. and Lambert Engines both went into receivership. During the court proceedings it took all of Don Luscombe's formidable sales skills to convince the judge to allow airplane manufacturing to continue. While a greatly reduced staff of key employees continued to tinker with clipped wings and other tricks to prepare Monocoupes for even more racing victories, the search was on for an investor with deep pockets. That investor turned out to be Phil De Cameron Ball, a St. Louis cold storage mogul who also owned the St. Louis Browns—and was stuck with a lot of worthless Mono-Aircraft stock.

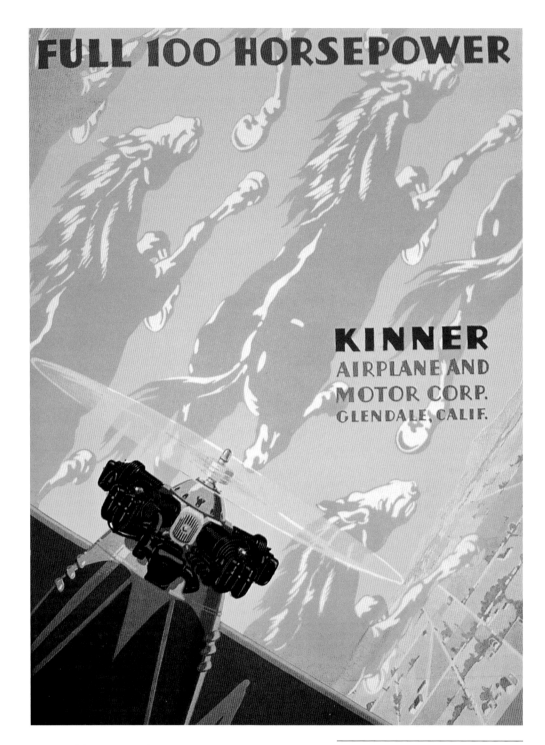

The 100-horsepower Kinner engine was a mainstay powerplant for sport aircraft. The colorful 1929 advertising got much blander the following year as the Depression struck, but Kinner was one of the survivors.

119

The Luscombe Phantom, Don Luscombe's attempt to take light aircraft manufacturing into the metal era. The complex monocoque fuselage and the rest of the airframe proved too expensive to produce after the failure of a mass production press required the parts to be handmade. The simplified production techniques developed from this experience made the Luscombe 8 a great success, however.

The Luscombe Phantom's two main wheels could get out of sync because of the independent struts and oleos and could make the airplane a bear to land in a crosswind.

De Cameron Ball asked Luscombe to stay on as general manager and move Mono-Aircraft into the old Ryan facility in St. Louis. The new company was renamed Monocoupe, and while its new benefactor wrote the checks to keep its doors open, it redoubled its efforts to sell airplanes again.

In 1930 the company introduced the Monocoupe 90, a highly cleaned-up and updated version of the popular Model 70, with a 90-horsepower Lambert engine encircled by a ring cowl. Its day would come, but it wasn't selling well when it first came on the market and was followed in a few months by a more powerful version equipped with a 110-horsepower Warner Scarab.

The Monocoupe 110, as this nimble airplane was called, became the darling of the racing community. It underwent all sorts of modifications, particularly in the hands of Johnny Livingston, and won the lion's share of many prizes claimed by Monocoupes.

The company's engineers decided to use the Model 110 as their point of departure and apply their experience with customizing it for racing to develop a certified super Monocoupe. This airplane was the Model D. It had a roomier cabin than its predecessors and was of the same mixed wood, fabric, and steel tube construction. But it was aerodynamically cleaner and more contemporary in appearance with its single strut gear, wheelpants, and NACA cowl. It was first equipped with a 125-horsepower Warner Scarab, which proved to be inadequate for the performance expected of the design. The engine was upgraded to a 145-horsepower Super Scarab, the vertical stabilizer was enlarged at the same time to cure some handling problems, and the airplane was called the D-145.

The D-145 had a cruise speed of 145 miles per hour, 1 mile per horsepower. It was unheard-of performance by a production light cabin monoplane, unmatched until the Cessna C-34 became available in 1935. But it was rightly reputed to be somewhat of a twitchy airplane, requiring a fine touch, especially on landing. Thus it didn't sell in large numbers, but developed a loyal following among a handful of its talented fans. Charles Lindbergh bought one of the 28 that were produced and absolutely loved it. On a visit to the aircraft manufacturers of Wichita, Kansas, with his wife, Anne Morrow, he ground looped it, apparently because of a stuck brake, and wiped out the landing gear and broke the two wingspars. But the frisky Monocoupe was soon repaired and returned to whisking Lucky Lindy along the airways at high speed on his inspection tours.

The D-145 was not certified until March 1934 and by then major changes had taken place at Monocoupe. First Fred Knoll, the chief engineer who was in charge of the D-145, left at the beginning of 1933 for reasons that may have been personal or related to what he perceived as interference by management with the airplane's design. His place was taken by the talented Ivan Driggs, who had specialized in light aircraft design and was highly respected in racing circles. Then came a major blow. Phil De Cameron Ball, Monocoupe's deep-pocketed benefactor, had a heart attack and died. Monocoupe's future was sud-

The Phantom's art deco cockpit was in line with standards of luxury for the time. Notice the typical central cluster of instruments equally accessible by both occupants.

ABOVE LEFT: The brass spark plug covers of the Warner Scarab are a nice touch.

The 125-horsepower Mescano-powered Ryan ST-A of the mid-1930s was a sporty open-cockpit monoplane, capable of graceful aerobatics. In inverted flight the flying wires sang because of the changed angle of attack. The fuselage was of monocoque construction, but the wings were braced by external wire. *Jim Koepnick/EAA*

denly uncertain. Don Luscombe, who had been close to De Cameron Ball, decided it was time to strike out on his own. He had an ambitious new airplane in mind and took Ivan Driggs with him to design it when he left Monocoupe at the end of 1933.

But Monocoupe survived the upheaval. It got the D-145 certified, and while that airplane had only a niche market, sales of the rest of the product line began to pick up nicely. In 1935 the company upgraded the Monocoupe 90 to the 90-A, which became its most popular model, a distinction the cheerful little airplane continues to enjoy in antique circles to this day.

The 90-A's chief improvements were a beautifully streamlined full NACA engine cowl with blisters for the rocker box covers and single strut gear with wheelpants, similar in style to the D-145. It could scoot along at 112 miles per hour on its 90 horsepower, burning a mere 5.5 gallons per hour and could keep it up for 550 miles on a tank of gas. At $3,485 it was the perfect sport airplane.

After a brief period of more musical chairs in Monocoupe's executive suite, by 1936 the well-liked Clare Burch, who had been in charge of sales, was running the company, and for the next few years Al Mooney was chief engineer.

When Don Luscombe left Monocoupe he moved to Kansas City and within days established the Luscombe Airplane Company. The airplane he was going to build required a daring leap of faith into modern metalworking technology. It would be a two-place, side-by-side, all-metal high-wing monoplane with a monocoque fuselage. Luscombe's plan was to make it available with a variety of engines, including the small cabin-class airplane's top-of-the-line engine choice, the 145-horsepower Warner Super Scarab.

It would be called the Phantom and would be one of the first airplanes to take light aircraft production into the new era of metal. Key to its success would be mass production, which, Luscombe was convinced,

The step beyond the steel tube framed fuselage. The monocoque fuselage of the Ryan ST-A eliminates the need for a load-carrying frame and dramatically cuts construction costs and time. The aluminum fuselage skin bears the load, saving weight and providing a more durable fuselage surface. *National Air and Space Museum*

The military picked up the Ryan ST-A as a primary trainer, eventually buying more than 1,200 in various versions. Here a flight of nine PT-22s, equipped with 160-horsepower Kinner engines (which were more reliable and powerful than the ST-A's Mescano), show how formation flying is done. *National Air and Space Museum*

neer of metal use in aircraft construction, it was a crude stretch press using end-wood maple forms to stamp out the compound curves of the Phantom's complex monocoque fuselage skins by the dozen in minutes.

Under Ivan Driggs' capable hand the development of the Phantom prototype progressed quickly, especially after several other associates of Luscombe at Monocoupe joined him in the new venture. It was built by hand while the Longren press was being readied for production and suitable formers were being made.

Luscombe convinced many friends, a number of whom owned Monocoupes, to invest in his company. An important financial backer was Aileen Brooks, the Bamberger Department Store heiress, whose equally privileged but less well-off husband, Peter Brooks, often demonstrated Monocoupes to his wealthy friends. Aileen was an outstanding pilot herself. She had flown a Monocoupe 90 on a round-trip between New York and Mexico City, and she and her husband went on an 18,000-mile honeymoon in "his" and "hers" Monocoupes.

As the Phantom began to take shape the emerging lines strongly evoked its Monocoupe heritage. It made its first flight in May 1934, and by August it was certified. At the National Air Races that year it was demonstrated as a noncompeting attendee and caused a sensation. It cruised at 145 miles per hour, but equally impressive to an audience used to wood and steel tube cages was its all-metal monocoque construction. The fuselage skins, riveted to a handful of bulkheads, were load bearing, forming an exceptionally strong, light, hollow fuselage.

In a splendid example of overengineering prompted by unfamiliarity with how metal will stand up to the rigors of flight, the Phantom was built like a tank. During the static tests 10 tons of sandbags were piled on the 150-pound monocoque fuselage to see how it would fare in the absence of a steel tube frame—there was nary a wrinkle. The wing also passed its load tests with flying colors. The Phantom was redlined at 240 miles per hour.

The strength of the Phantom's airframe quickly became the stuff of legend. One Luscombe board member had his Phantom painted in the metallic bronze color of the can of his favorite beer. Then with a great deal of audacity and little common sense he decided to see just how high a Phantom would go. The last thing he remembered about the ascent was being very high in more ways than one. He regained consciousness to find the airplane in a shrieking dive, close to the ground as the airspeed needle swung past 300 miles per hour. He pulled out somewhat overzeal-

The 1938 Cessna C-38 got a bow leg to increase the wheelbase, a belly flap, and was the first to be called the Airmaster, a name retroactively applied to the entire line. *Jim Koepnick/EAA*

would allow him to offer the airplane for as low as $3,000. Don Luscombe had seen the future and it was the Phantom. And it would go like a bat out of hell—Luscombe could just feel it in his bones.

To implement his plans for mass production Luscombe planned to rely heavily on the capabilities of the Longren press. The creation of A. K. Longren, a pio-

The open-cockpit Waco soldiered on as the cabin class took over. In 1930 Waco introduced the F series, a smaller, more economical version of its open-cockpit biplane, which remained in production throughout the 1930s. Pictured is a Waco QCF-2. *Carl Schuppel/EAA*

The Parks biplane already looked obsolete when it came on the scene at the end of the 1920s. It was built by Parks College as a trainer for its students, hence the basic nature of the airplane. The Parks and airplanes like it that were no longer produced in the 1930s kept on flying in the hands of pilots on a budget. The airplane pictured is the one author Richard Bach flew across the country and wrote about it in *Biplane*.

Meanwhile In Europe

While personal and business aviation thrived in North America, the light aircraft industry was also making commendable progress across the Atlantic, following, in some respects, a different path. Although it can be risky to generalize, it may be safely said that throughout the European flying community there has been a greater tendency toward relying more on aerodynamic efficiency to achieve desired results rather than on brute power.

In the United States the answer to the quest for high performance was often, "Let's hang the biggest engine on it that we can find and do the best we can with the airframe to carry it." In Europe more often than not (especially in the case of light aircraft), the thinking was, "We have a given engine that is affordable and reasonably economical to operate, so let's do all we can with the airframe to get the most aerodynamic performance possible out of it."

In England personal aviation got its first big boost during the second half of the 1920s with the introduction in 1925 of Geoffrey de Havilland's famous Moths. De Havilland already had a distinguished record including the design of the World War I DH-4 biplane, which was widely used in the United States as a mail plane. The Moth was a light wood-and-fabric biplane for which de Havilland had to develop its own engine because there wasn't a suitable one available. This four-cylinder 60-horsepower inline engine was called the Cirrus (variants were license-produced in the United States). Within two years it was followed by the 85-horsepower Gypsy engines, derivatives of which went on to supply virtually the entire British light aircraft industry into the 1950s.

Britain's intrepid sports fliers lost little time in setting out on the most audacious flights in their little Cirrus Moths, Gypsy Moths, and the aircraft that followed. Flights to British possessions overseas were especially popular. Sir Francis Chicester's epic journey from England to Australia in 1929 in his Gypsy Moth started a trend for the following decade. Personal flights down to eastern and southern Africa also became quite common. A little known fact is that more than 200 Gypsy Moths were produced in the United States in Lowell, Massachusetts, under license.

De Havilland's most famous Moth was the DH 82A Tiger Moth, powered by a 135-horsepower Gypsy Major. Like the Boeing Model 75 that everyone knows as THE Stearman, it came late in the biplane's evolution, making its debut in 1933. But like the Stearman, it was picked up as its nation's primary trainer, and more than 8,000 were made on four continents (many were built in Canada).

De Havilland was also responsible for building one of the more famous air-racing airplanes, the twin-engined DH 88 Comet. A red-and-white Comet won the 1934 MacRobertson race from England to Australia. The sleek Comet with its two inline 230-horsepower Gypsy Six engines was quite a different animal from the 710-horsepower monster Staggerwing that Walter Beech had built for Louise Thaden to fly in the MacRobertson race (she stayed home due to lack of funding).

During the 1930s a notable development in personal aircraft design in Europe was the emergence of several beautiful low-wing cantilever cabin monoplanes, including the Percival Vega Gull.

The Belgian-French Stampe was another European biplane destined to become a popular antique, but it was even more of an anachronism by the time it appeared in 1936 than either the Tiger Moth or the Boeing-Stearman. Superficially it resembled a Tiger Moth, but it was a completely different and much better handling airplane, renown for its aerobatic abilities. Made only in limited quantities before the war, it was mass produced by the French government in the late 1940s and became a favorite with flying clubs. Even today, there is a Stampe Class on the European aerobatic competition circuit.

In Germany the development of efficient, low-powered light aircraft was further boosted by the severe restrictions imposed by the Versailles Treaty on power flying. Gliding mushroomed as a result and with it a reverence for aerodynamics that well served the designers of the low-powered aircraft such as the Klemm monoplane when the Germans began testing how far they could go in abusing the Versailles restrictions. Besides several aerodynamically advanced low-wing touring monoplanes made by such well-known companies as Messerschmitt and Arado, during the 1930s Germany also gave the world two of the feistiest aerobatic biplanes, the Bücker Jungmeister and Jungman. A Vibrant European antique movement keeps all of these Old World airplanes alive today.

De Havilland Comet and Dragon Rapide formation. Jim Koepnick/EAA

FAR LEFT: Bücker Jungmeister.

LEFT: The oldest DH-82 Tiger Moth flying with the Tiger Club of England.

TOP: Bill King'sTiger Moth and Gene DeMarco's Stampe SV.4B formation.

ABOVE: Dragon Rapide. Jim Koepnick/EAA

Airport scene, circa 1935: a Stearman C-3 is being refueled, and a Douglas DC-2 and Curtiss Robin are in the background. Note the pilot's cigar. Presumably he put it out. *National Air and Space Museum*

ously and badly buckled the wing's leading edge, but the Phantom somehow kept flying. He totaled it in a crash landing in an apple orchard but walked away without a scratch.

Joseph Juptner has called the Phantom a love affair designed for the accomplished pilot and the wealthy sportsman. Unfortunately, he pointed out, the accomplished pilot was not always wealthy and the wealthy sportsman was not always accomplished. One weakness of the Phantom that caused Juptner to fear for the unaccomplished wealthy sportsman was its narrow, super-sensitive landing gear. The gear strut's independent oleos could get rapidly out of sync if the wheels weren't perfectly aligned with the runway on landing, setting up the ideal conditions for a severe ground loop. If an agitated pilot reacted by braking too hard there was a real danger of nosing over.

Don Luscombe liked to say that you could master the violin more easily than the fancy footwork required to avoid ground looping.

Luscombe himself flipped a Phantom on its back while demonstrating it to a potential client from Switzerland. She was so impressed by not being injured and the minor damage sustained by the Phantom that she placed a deposit for one on the spot. Unfortunately her check turned out to be the exception, not the rule.

The Phantom wasn't selling. The Longren press in which Luscombe had invested so much faith turned out to be a dud. It destroyed nine out of ten skins that were fed into it. Luscombe should have gotten the hint from the fact that it bankrupted its inventor, but the future looked too promising to let such thoughts

intrude. The only alternative to the press was to have Nick Nordyke, Luscombe Airplane's artist with the pneumatic hammer, form every piece by hand.

The Phantom went from the promise of mass production to being one of the most labor-intensive airplanes to be built. Luscombe barely broke even at the $6,000 price he felt compelled to ask for it, but it was too high to attract the number of buyers the company needed. He even moved the factory to New Jersey to be closer to his moneyed East Coast clientele, but to no avail. Only 22 Phantoms were sold between 1934 and 1941.

But Don Luscombe learned his lessons and poured them into his next all-metal monocoque airplane, which in its final version would truly lead light aircraft building into a new era—and inspire Cessna to develop an airplane after World War II that would be a major league home run.

A cabin-class airplane of the 1930s that started out small and proved far better at attracting customers than the Phantom was the Fairchild 24. It was introduced in 1931 as the Model 24 C-8, a side-by-side 90-horsepower two-seater, but would grow into a 175-horsepower four-seater through a series of 16 model upgrades, which were so incremental that the basic model designation would never be changed.

The Fairchild 24 was a thoroughly conventional wood, fabric, and steel tube design, with a strong resemblance to the larger Stinson SM Junior and later, to a lesser degree, the straight-winged Reliant. In a manner similar to Waco's approach to designing the Cabin Waco, the Kreider Reisner division of Fairchild developed the Model 24 from its tandem open-cockpit Model 22 (discussed later in this chapter).

Two relatively unusual features of the first Fairchild 24 were full span ailerons and its American Cirrus "Hi-Drive" engine. The Cirrus was an inverted inline four-cylinder powerplant of British origin built in the United States under license. It was one of the first attempts to devise a more streamlined alternative to the drag-laden radial engine for light aircraft.

Although the little Cirrus served some airplanes well, the Fairchild 24 was not one of them. The 24's relatively large and not particularly streamlined airframe needed more power. For the 1933 model year it got 125 horsepower in two versions: the C-8A, equipped with a Warner Scarab radial, and the C-8B with an inline Mescano C4. Fairchild salesmen pushed the Warner-powered version, and consequently only two F 24s were built with the Mescano. But more than any other manufacturer, Fairchild continued to offer many subsequent F 24 models with both radial and inline engines.

This Fairchild 24W demonstrates the capabilities of golden age airplanes, old as it may seem today. It was one of hundreds used by the RAF as liaison airplanes, which found its way down to South Africa. It was purchased and restored there in the 1980s by Chalkie Stoddard. In 1992 Chalkie and his friend Peter Hengst flew the Fairchild from South Africa to Oshkosh, Wisconsin, for the EAA convention. The trip took 125 hours through Europe and over the North Atlantic. *Carl Schuppel/EAA*

This flight instrument advertisement shows an interesting Monocoupe and Stinson Reliant line-up. The instrument display is quite basic for 1937, when blind flying instruments were already available.

The Ryan ST-A's military trainer version, the Kinner-powered PT-22. More than 1,000 were purchased by the armed forces. The military found the Mescano engine not up to the abuse of intensive training flights, hence the switch to the Kinner.

In 1934 the Fairchild 24 was so substantially upgraded that a new model designation would have made perfect sense, but it remained the 24. The fuselage was enlarged, the wing area was increased, the wing struts were changed from a parallel to a V layout, and the full-span ailerons were reduced in length and changed to Frieze ailerons. Most interesting from the owners' point of view was the addition of a third "rumble" seat in the back.

To haul the new, larger airframe around, the engine was upgraded to the 145-horsepower Super Scarab. This version was known as the C8C. It is interesting to compare this Fairchild's performance with the Cessna C-34, which had the same engine and seated four. The Fairchild cruised at 120 miles per hour and had a useful load of 796 pounds. The Cessna C-34 cruised at 143 miles per hour with a useful load of 980 pounds. The Fairchild landed at 49 miles per hour, the Cessna at 54 miles per hour. Both aircraft had about a 500-mile range. If you wanted the Cessna's extra performance it would cost you an extra $1,000 over the Fairchild's $4,000 price tag.

The price certainly had something to do with the great popularity of the Fairchild 24 C8C of which more than 100 were produced during 1934 and 1935, which is more than *all* models of the Cessna Airmaster ever made. It wasn't only money. The entire Fairchild series was well loved by private owners because it was one of the most forgiving, pleasant airplanes to fly.

In 1935 the Fairchild 24 was equipped with trailing edge flaps. It was also offered with a 145-horsepower inline six-cylinder Ranger, an engine developed by Fairchild in-house. The Ranger installation got a lot of attention and was even exhibited at the International Air Show in Milan, Italy. Yet its performance wasn't any different from its Scarab-equipped stablemate's, and it didn't sell nearly as well.

In 1938 Fairchild finally took the obvious step and upgraded the 24 to a four-seater. It was available with two engines, the trusty 145-horsepower Scarab (the C8-J) and a 165-horsepower Ranger (the C8-K). The market voted for the higher powered Ranger; 60 C8-Ks were sold compared to 11 Js. Changes were minor for the remainder of the 24's civilian production life prior to World War II.

The Fairchild 24 line sold in the hundreds because it was the ideal choice for the sport pilot who wanted a little more speed and a lot more cabin room than the smaller Monocoupes had to offer, and didn't want to have anything to do with a "hot ship" such as the 145-horsepower Monocoupe or the more expensive large cabin class.

When war came the Fairchild 24 found itself in greater demand than it had been during its entire civilian history. The U.S. armed forces purchased 984 of them, many equipped with a 200-horsepower Ranger that was never offered on the civilian market. It was also popular with Britain's Royal Air Force, which bought 161 of them outright and 364 under the Lend Lease program. (The British designations were Argus I and III. They were used for liaison duties and to retrieve ferry pilots.) Many of these airplanes have found their way back onto the civilian market and are valued antiques today.

A sportsman pilot of the mid-1930s looking for a small budget, cabin-class airplane along the lines of the Monocoupe 70 rather than the Fairchild 24 had two other interesting choices, the Rearwin Sportster and the Porterfield Flyabout. Powered initially by 70-horsepower LeBlond radial engines followed by more powerful engine options, the two looked and performed remarkably alike, with a small range advantage to the Sportster, which also acquired a reputation for being better made.

Rae Rearwin and Ed Porterfield used a design for these two aircraft that was developed by engineer Noel Hockaday, who worked for both of them in pre-Depression days. In 1933, with little to do, Hockaday designed a light high-wing tandem monoplane along early Taylorcraft lines, which the shop students at Kansas City's Wyandotte High School built as a project. Powered by an obscure three-cylinder 30-horsepower Poyer engine, it was called the Wyandotte Pup. It was seized by both Rearwin and Porterfield as the way back into the airplane business—suitably developed, it would easily become a capable enclosed sport airplane that sold for between $1,700 and 2,500.

Ed Porterfield started up a company specifically to develop the Pup and convinced Hockaday to join him as chief engineer and general manager. Rae Rearwin was working through Rearwin Aircraft, the company he set up independently of the pre-Depression Rearwin Airplanes (whose other major stockholders wanted to keep the old company dormant, but did not object to Rearwin's new venture). Besides direct inspiration, the Sportster also owed its

In 1939 Fairchild was positioning its Ranger-powered F-24 to the private owner market. By then the airplane had become a highly popular private four-seater.

resemblance to the Pup to the influence of Hockaday's work on earlier Rearwins when he was employed by the company. In the incestuous little world of Kansas City aviation, Porterfield and Rearwin became "spirited" competitors.

Both airplanes were of traditional wood, fabric, and steel tube construction, and more than a hundred were made of both models with the Rearwin holding a slight lead in sales. Cruising at anywhere from 105 to 120 miles per hour depending on the version, both the Flyabout and the Sportster line were indeed popular with sports fliers and flying schools. Louise Thaden briefly raced a Porterfield for fun. Juan Trippe, founder and CEO of Pan American World Airways, kept a Rearwin Sportster on floats on Long Island Sound and occasionally used it to commute to Pan Am's Manhattan headquarters, landing on the East River.

Porterfield was content to stick to the Flyabout, but Rearwin had other plans. To move beyond the Sportster, the company developed the Cloudster, but it wasn't certified until 1939. It was developed from a sleek but troubled tandem design called the Speedster, which initially had an American Cirrus and then a 125-horsepower Mescano engine. The Speedster was Rearwin's first airplane after the Depression, but was

The Waco UPF-7 was the last of the open-cockpit Wacos, and also one of the most numerous. Produced until 1942, 600 were delivered to the military as primary trainers for the Civilian Pilot Training Program. It is a popular and widely available antique.

plagued with difficulties attempting to pass its spin tests. When it was finally certified in 1937 its sales were sluggish. Rearwin decided to improve on it to produce the Cloudster and in the process created a considerably different and much better airplane.

Seating was changed from tandem configuration to side-by-side seats, the airframe was scaled up, and the airplane got a NACA cowl. It looked outstanding, resembling a mini-cabin Howard DGA, especially with wheelpants. Power initially came from a 90-horsepower Ken-Royce (formerly LeBlond) radial engine, which was soon upgraded to 120 horsepower.

The Cloudster was a lovely recreational airplane, but unfortunately it appeared too late on the scene to realize its potential. By the time it was certified in October 1939 there had been several other aircraft of similar performance on the market for several years, and civilian aviation was running out of time.

Nevertheless, Rearwin did sell about 125 Cloudsters, many of them as trainers, including 25 to the National Aeroclub of Iran and 5 to Pan American for instrument training. The Pan Am Cloudsters were modified to tandem seating with a full set of instruments in the front and rear. Similar training aircraft

The Fairchild 24 also had a distinguished military career. This 1937 F-24G was co-opted into the Civil Air Patrol and more than 1,000 F-24s were made specifically for the war.

were also sold to various flying schools. The Pan Am purchase was undoubtedly influenced by Juan Trippe's experience with his Sportster. Today the cabin Rearwins are among the rarest antiques.

Although the heyday of the open-cockpit biplane had passed by the 1930s, sport pilots with a yen to fly a current production airplane and feel the wind in their face could always buy an open-cockpit Waco. Two basic models of the open-cockpit Waco were produced after the turn of the decade, the sporty F series and the more unusual A series. The F series was a continuation of the traditional three-seat open-cockpit Waco, but scaled down to accommodate the option of smaller engines and realize greater economies of operation. In the typical Waco manner it was offered with a salad bar of engines over the years.

The F series remained in production until 1942 because of the UPF-7, which was introduced in 1938. It was developed explicitly with primary pilot training in mind and became very popular when the Civilian Pilot Training Program got under way in 1939. This program's intent was to rapidly produce a large pool of basically trained pilots on government subsidy as a precaution against a sudden military need. Waco made some 600 UPF-7s for the program, and understandably they are the most numerous survivors today.

Optimized for training, the UPF-7 was slightly beefier than the previous F models. Powered by a seven-cylinder 220-horsepower Continental, it originally had only one seat up front instead of two.

The A series Waco was an unusual side-by-side two-seater convertible. To fly with their hair let down the pilots could leave the canopy on the ground. To make it to important business engagements with their hair in place they could fly with the canopy installed. The Model A was Waco's attempt to woo back pilots being seduced away from the open-cockpit biplane by the cabin class. It, too, was available with a range of engines.

The open Wacos were lovely biplanes, but pilots preferring a smaller, open-cockpit monoplane also had several alternatives. The most interesting of these was without a doubt the Ryan ST.

T. Claude Ryan had sold his interest in the company that made the *Spirit of St. Louis*, and by the early 1930s he was operating a flying school in San Diego. His experience with the school gave him the idea that he could develop a better trainer than the Great Lakes biplanes he was using. Ryan admired the P-26 fighter and the efficiency of the small, fast racers of the time. He was impressed by the all-metal commercial aircraft coming onto the scene, and he recognized the potential of metal

construction for mass production. Inspired by these factors, in 1933 he formed a new company, the Ryan Aeronautical Company, and developed the Ryan ST.

ST stood for Sport Trainer, and it was a trainer like no other before it. A sleek, low-wing, tandem open-cockpit monoplane with a 95-horsepower Mescano B-4 inline engine, it was made of metal except for its wooden wing spars. Its monocoque fuselage had only eight bulkheads to support the aluminum stressed skin. It had no compound curves, only straight sheet metal curled around the bulkheads, lending itself to fast, low-cost production. Aluminum fairings smoothed out the mating of the airframe components.

The wings were a bit more old-fashioned. Although the ribs were aluminum, the spars were made of spruce and it wasn't a cantilever design, requiring struts and flying wires for structural support (the flying wires whistled like banshees in inverted flight because of the changed angle of attack). The wings were equipped with flaps, a rarity in trainers of the day but necessitated by a relatively high wing loading and the attendant high landing speeds. The faired fixed landing gear was straight off the Gee Bee–type racers.

As is often the case with new designs, the Ryan ST soon got an upgraded engine. The original airplane was certified in 1934, but within a year it was re-engined with a 125-horsepower Mescano. This model was designated the ST-A and was the one that went into mass production.

The Ryan ST was designed as a trainer, but it also appealed strongly to the sportsman pilot. It was the closest an adventurous weekend warrior could come to flying a fighter like the P-26 without joining up, or to emulating safely the experience of flying the thoroughbred racers that so captured the imagination. It was also suitable for aerobatics. In 1937, Tex Rankin, one the founders of competition aerobatics in America, won the National Aerobatic Competition in his 150-horsepower supercharged Mescano-equipped Ryan, which was known as the ST-A Special.

The Ryan ST-A cruised at 127 miles per hour on its 125-horsepower engine, had a range of 350 miles, and sold for around $4,500. In a novel arrangement an extra fuel tank could be slipped onto the front seat, which nearly doubled endurance. For solo flying the front seat opening could be covered with a fairing to marginally reduce drag and give the airplane a single-seat appearance.

With such credentials the ST-A was a strong candidate in the U.S. Army Air Corps' primary trainer competition in 1939. The military was sufficiently

An aerial posse across the hazy
Iowa farm country, 1930s style. A
Stinson Detroiter leads the Ryan
ST-A while two open-cockpit
biplanes bring up the rear.
P. Michael Whyte/AAA

The Great Lakes sport biplane went out of production in 1933 but continued to provide many hours of aerobatic pleasure to adventurous sport pilots who still preferred to feel the wind on their cheeks.

The major modification for military use was the replacement of the Mescano, which was a rather sensitive engine that didn't stand up to much abuse, with the more reliable and rugged 132-horsepower Kinner radial. The Kinner was nicely faired in with a bullet-like cowl that had cut-outs for the cylinder heads, and the conversion worked well in spite of the slight extra drag. The Mescano-powered military ST-A was designated the PT-16, the Kinner-powered version the PT16A.

Other changes recommended by the evaluation included enlarging the cockpit openings, so that military pilots with all their gear could clamber in and out of the airplane more easily, and losing the wheel fairings, which were more trouble than they were worth from a maintenance standpoint in intensive military training use.

An initial batch of 40 Ryans entered regular military service with the modifications except the engine change, as the PT-20. Most were soon converted to the Kinner and designated the PT-20A. These modest orders were followed by one for 200 (100 each for the Army and Navy), for which the airframe was slightly redesigned to military specs, incorporating a wider wheelbase and a modified empennage. These airplanes were designated the PT-21 (NR-1 in the Navy). The engine was then upgraded to a 160-horsepower Kinner. This version of the airplane became the PT-22 and more than 1,000 of them were bought by the armed forces.

impressed to place an initial order for 15 airplanes and put them through a comprehensive service evaluation process. The tests revealed some easily correctable weaknesses, and larger orders followed.

The Rearwin Sportster was a relatively popular tandem two-seat recreational airplane of the mid-1930s, cruising as fast as 120 miles per hour. Juan Trippe kept a Sportster on floats on Long Island Sound and occasionally used it to commute to Manhattan. *National Air and Space Museum*

Brief mention should also be made of Ryan's modern cabin sport monoplane developed alongside the ST series and introduced in 1937. Appropriately named the Sport Cabin, it was an all-metal airplane with side-by-side seating, a monocoque fuselage, and an interesting, stressed-skin monospar wing that was very advanced for this type of aircraft. In looks the Sport Cabin resembled some designs in Europe, where the low-wing, efficient monoplane concept was popular, but the airframe technology was ahead of them. Powered by a 145 Warner Scarab (after initial experiments with an inline Mescano) the SC had a top speed of 140 miles per hour and cruised at 125 miles per hour. Only 10 Sport Cabins were built, perhaps because of Ryan's growing commitments for military work.

Returning to the open-cockpit monoplanes, an alternative to the Ryan ST for sportsman pilots of the more sedentary type was the high-wing Fairchild 22. Introduced in 1931 by the Kreider Reisner division of Fairchild, it was of conventional construction and had full-span ailerons. Its wing arrangement looked as if someone had forgotten the lower wing of a set of biplane wings, and it was sometimes referred to as a parasol wing. Powered mostly by a variety of inline engines including the 90-horsepower American Cirrus and 125-horsepower Mescano, it had a graceful-looking fuselage, except for some pug-nosed F 22s that were equipped with Scarab radials toward the end of the line's 200-plus production run.

The aircraft of the 1930s that fell into the 70- to 145-horsepower category opened up the world of flying to countless pilots who wanted more from an airplane than what the utilitarian Piper Cubs and their kin could provide, but weren't in the Staggerwing league. The Airmasters, Fairchilds, Monocoupes, Rearwins, Porterfields, Ryans, and the Phantom were the soul of the sportsman pilot's world during the golden age; but in the aftermath of World War II, their time was past. There were a few false starts to revive some of them, but soon they were all out of production for good, their place taken by a more efficient, less costly breed, which owed its development to the light, flat-four engine and took its cue from the humble Cub, Taylorcraft, and Aeronca.

Wings Of Change

As the 1930s progressed, Lindbergh's infectious spirit thrived. Aviation was the cutting-edge technology of the age. The public's fascination with flying warranted the maintenance of fully staffed aviation desks at all the major newspapers. The economy was inching its way back to health, and the cost of flying and aircraft ownership for pleasure and business was again becoming affordable to an increasing number of people and corporations. From the mid-1930s personal aircraft production numbers began to suggest assembly-line operations instead of small-scale custom building.

As we've seen, the cabin class had come to dominate personal aviation across the board, with a wide range of exciting aircraft available, from the luxurious behemoths capable of outrunning any airplane the airlines had to offer, to solid little cross-country trundlers for the recreational pilot with more modest aspirations.

But these aircraft were still too expensive except for the particularly well heeled. As the Depression eased, more middle class people had money to spend on more than the basics, but nowhere near the resources available to the sportsman crowd. Yet aviation's hold on them was just as powerful. Aeronca and Taylor Aircraft, the two firms that had stayed the course of the so-called flivver plane era, saw an increasing opportunity for making money on their bargain-priced very light aircraft. Yet they continued to be plagued by the lack of a sufficiently light but powerful and reliable engine to give these airplanes more than marginal performance.

In 1930 Aeronca was manufacturing its own 40-horsepower two-stroke engine for the C-2 "Bathtub," and Taylor Aircraft was rather desperately casting about for an engine for its E-2.

The E-2 managed only to hop with C. G. Taylor's first choice, the 20-horsepower Tiger Kitten. But it did prompt one of Taylor's colleagues to remark that if the engine was called Tiger Kitten then the E-2 should surely be called the Cub, and so a name was born. A beautifully crafted, tiny nine-cylinder French Salmson 40 radial was tried and rejected as too expensive,

The Piper Cub. Taylor's airplane had become a Piper and the original J-3's 65-horsepower flat-four engine enabled it to blossom for a fraction of the cost of radial-engined sport airplanes. In 1939, 6,000 Cubs were made for the Civilian Pilot Training Program, and later another 6,000 were made for the war followed by about 10,000 in the post-war years. *Martin Berinstein*

The little engine that could. Continental's introduction of the 40-horsepower A-40 horizontally opposed flat-four engine was the beginning of the end for the radial in personal aviation. The engine soon grew in power to 65 horsepower (pictured) and beyond.

139

weight specification of 850 pounds could hope for and was bolted eagerly to the E-2's nose.

Not all went smoothly with the engine in the beginning. Taylor is quoted as saying that in the first 30 days of flying with the A-40 the E-2 had to make 26 forced landings, and as service experience increased, it was discovered that the crankshaft tended to break at around 100 hours. But Continental worked hard to resolve the bugs, and the engine eventually functioned acceptably. Nevertheless, with only 37 horsepower it froze the development potential of the Taylor Cub until a more powerful version of the flat-four engine became available.

Little progress was made in the further development of the Continental or the E-2 for the next few years. Taylor Cub sales were under 25 per year through 1933, but tripled the next year, indicative of the recovering economy.

In late 1935 Taylor and Piper had a nasty parting of the ways. In what appears to have been a personality clash between two strong-willed men, Piper essentially forced out Taylor, who didn't hang his head for long. He shortly set up a new company called Taylorcraft and began developing the Taylorcraft Model A.

Unsurprisingly Taylor's new design was a cleaned-up E-2 with side-by-side seating, powered by the same Continental A-40. Its fully enclosed cabin structure flowed straight aft from the wing, eliminating the E-2's awkward faired-in parasol wing look. For a brief time Taylorcraft was in Butler, Pennsylvania, before moving to permanent quarters in Alliance, Ohio. The Model A received group 2 approval in late 1936 and was certified in mid-1937.

Just as Taylorcraft was setting up in Butler, Piper introduced the J-2. It was called a Taylor J-2 because Piper was keeping the Taylor Aircraft Company name for the time being to maintain marketing continuity during the transition from the E-2. The new Cub benefited from a significant airframe improvement over the E-2 and, except for the tandem seating, it was uncannily similar to what the Model A was going to be. The cabin was fully enclosed with a continuous sweep of the fuselage aft of the wing and the wingtips and tail surfaces were pleasingly rounded off. The J-2 also retained the A-40 Continental.

As Taylor and Piper prepared to go head-to-head, the market heated up for the ultralight airplanes they made. The middle class was finally learning to fly and flying schools clamored for the friendly little Cub priced at only $1,470, with only $490 down and a year to pay off the balance, during which it could be put to work to earn the payments.

Piper J-3 Cub maneuvering over scenic terrain. *National Air and Space Museum*

Piper aggressively promoted training use, throwing in a free flight course with every purchase. Only $425 down was needed to purchase a Cub. The rest could be paid off in a year, allowing flight schools to make the Cub pay for itself.

although it performed well on the E-2.

Then Taylor and his partner, William Piper, found what would prove to be the first of a new breed of light aircraft engines, the Continental A-40. A 37-horsepower air-cooled four-cylinder engine, it was just then going into production. Its cylinders were laid out in a horizontally opposed configuration, a characteristic that has led to such engines being commonly referred to as "flat fours." Aluminum was extensively used in the A-40, and it weighed only 137 pounds. It held all the promise that a design with a gross

The Luscombe 8, the first successful modern metal personal light airplane. Luscombe learned the lessons from the Phantom and devised a simple monocoque fuselage structure that could be easily mass produced. Coupled with the 50-horsepower Continental A-50 engine, the Luscombe 8 was a winner.

Luscombe 8.*National Air and Space Museum*

In 1936 Piper sold 550 J-2s, including the 1,000th Cub to be built since the E-2's debut. The following year J-2 sales jumped to 658, and the price was reduced to $1,270. An even greater number of J-2s would have been made to meet demand, but production was held back by a crippling fire at the plant. The fire prompted the company to relocate from Bradford into a defunct textile mill in a town called Lock Haven, Pennsylvania, and officially change its name to the Piper Aircraft Corporation.

Taylorcraft began selling the Model A only in 1937, yet by August it had delivered its 200th airplane. These figures weren't lost on Aeronca or the engine manufacturers. Aeronca introduced the Model K, sort of a C-3 that had sprouted gear struts and got an airframe makeover. A side-by-side two-seater, it was powered by Aeronca's in-house 40-horsepower two-cylinder engine. It looked and flew remarkably like the Taylorcraft Model A and the Piper J-2, and about 350 of them were sold in the next two years.

Faced with such demand the engine manufacturers were about to come up with an engine that would

Taylorcraft and all the other aircraft of similar design were available with the various competing light flat-four engines that were coming on the market, such as the 50-horsepower Lycoming 145.

prove to be a breakthrough in performance, the 50-horsepower flat four. Continental was upgrading the A-40 to the A-50. Lycoming was going into the flat four business with the O-145, and Franklin was offering the 4AC-150.

Attaining the 50-horsepower threshold was important given the absolute limits of making light, structurally sound airframes. Fifty horsepower was the minimum power required to carry two people in such an airframe with a consistently safe climb rate, and at reasonable speed and range that would transform these machines from little more than powered gliders into useful aircraft.

The aircraft manufacturers couldn't get enough of the new engines and offered new airplane models with a choice of them. Piper's J-3, an improved J-2 originally introduced with the 40-horsepower Continental, came out with a choice of each of the 50-horsepower engines. Taylorcraft brought out the Model B with the new powerplants, and Aeronca upgraded the Model K to the 50-horsepower Chief.

In 1938, Piper was feeling some pressure from the market to come up with a side-by-side seat version of the Cub to directly match Taylorcraft's Model B and the Aeronca Chief. In response the company intro-

The Aeronca Chief was a descendant of the C-3 Flying Bathtub and a competitor of the Taylorcraft and the Cub Coupe. As was the case with the OX-5-powered New Swallow, the Travel Air, and the Waco 10 two decades before, it was difficult to tell the difference between the 65-horsepower flat-four-equipped fleet. As before, differences would emerge with an increase in engine performance.

Of the large cabin-class manufacturers, only Stinson took up the flat-four challenge and was quite successful with the little Voyager, drawing a parallel with its big brother, the Reliant.

$2995*

STINSON 1939 "RELIANT"

See the new 1939 Stinson "Reliant". All the famous features which have won such tremendous preference for this plane among sportsmen, businessmen, government agencies and airlines are incorporated plus more speed, more comfort and more luxury. The new Reliant has 25 new improvements.

duced the J-4 Cub Coupe, initially with the Continental A-50 engine. It was a perky little machine, and Piper marketed it aggressively as a luxury airplane.

Borrowing the automotive pitch from the large cabin class, the company went out of its way to equate the J-4 with everyman's friendly automobile. First, there was the name, Coupe. Then there were the gracefully curved lines adorned with automotive-style grillework. In sharp contrast to the utilitarian tandem Cubs, its cabin was plushly upholstered. The instrument panel looked like the dashboard of a Chevrolet, complete with ignition key and rear-view mirror. You could roll down the window, stick out your elbow, and cruise across the countryside all Sunday afternoon.

As they gained service experience the capable flat-four engines were given a power boost to 65 horsepower, which was enthusiastically embraced by their market. At that power output they were also becoming a viable alternative to the heavier, draggy, 70-plus horsepower radials powering the Monocoupes, Porterfields, and Rearwins. Soon they were going to get even more powerful. It was only a matter of time before the flat four would displace the radial as the engine of choice in personal aviation.

When the manufacturers raised the small flat-four engine's power output to 50 horsepower, one aircraft maker who paid attention was Don Luscombe. Taking the Phantom's lessons to heart he had thrown himself into the next project he perceived to be the future of aviation, and this time he was right—it was the airplane that would evolve into the Luscombe Model 8.

While his employees custom crafted the few expensive Phantoms that were being ordered, Don Luscombe kept the bills paid by running a highly acclaimed mechanic's school, the Luscombe School of Aviation, by persuading investors to keep buying into the company, and at one point even by doing subcontract work for Pitcairn's autogyro. But to make it as an aircraft manufacturer he badly needed an airplane that would sell.

In 1936 he instigated the design of the Luscombe 90. It was to be a less expensive airplane based on the Phantom, powered by a 90-horsepower Scarab, and constructed with cost-saving simplified building techniques. The first crack at a prototype 90 was essentially a modified Phantom with a tamed landing gear configuration and the 90-horsepower engine. It was a dog.

Luscombe and his engineers concluded that a new, much lighter and simpler airframe needed to be designed from scratch. Chief engineer Lyle Farver, who had been groomed by Ivan Driggs (now at Martin), and his assistants began to develop a simple

monocoque fuselage with no compound curves. Flat aluminum sheets were bent around and riveted to stamped bulkheads, similar to the Ryan ST fuselage.

As the design of the 90 progressed, Luscombe became concerned that it would be too expensive to operate with the Scarab for the type of airplane it was going to be. He began to think seriously for the first time of a smaller metal airplane, similar to the wood, fabric, and steel tube Cubs and Aeroncas. If it could be produced for less with labor-saving metalworking techniques, but would have equal or better performance, it would be a winner. And he had a novel idea for fleshing out the concept. He would get the Luscombe School of Aviation to tackle it as a student project.

The students set to work under the guidance of their instructor, Frank Johnson. They came up with a design and built a fuselage mockup that demonstrated how work-saving features could be applied to inexpensively construct a perky little, competitive side-by-side metal two-seater with a fabric-covered high aspect ratio wing. It had the lines of the Cub and the Aeronca and was proposed with the 40-horsepower Continental A-40 or the more powerful, but at the time still experimental, A-50.

Luscombe liked the airplane, but he was initially ambivalent because he mistrusted the engine. When he

As the war came to a close, manufacturers were optimistically predicting a personal airplane in every garage. Returning GIs would flock to get their pilot's licenses under the GI bill, it was predicted, and the assembly lines began to roll with vengeance. A postwar recession temporarily put a damper on the rosy forecasts, but in coming decades personal aircraft would be sold by the tens of thousands per year. *National Air and Space Museum*

WHEN IS A STEARMAN NOT A STEARMAN?

When is a Stearman not a Stearman? When it is a Boeing Kaydet. The lovely large open-cockpit military biplane that has become the stereotype Stearman entered service long after Lloyd Stearman sold his company to the giant United Aircraft conglomerate in 1929 and left for other adventures. United Aircraft also owned Boeing. When the government broke up United Aircraft on antitrust grounds in 1934, Boeing was one of the companies to go. It took Stearman along as a subsidiary and converted it into the Wichita Division of Boeing in 1939.

The Stearman's official name was the Boeing Model 75. It didn't enter service until 1935, long after the biplane's heyday had passed. By all accounts it should have had a limited life, but war once again intervened and more than 8,500 of them were built as primary trainers for the Army Air Corps and the Navy. Being flying brick outhouses, it was a role for which they were eminently suited. Their Army Air Corps designation is PT-13, with the 220-horsepower Lycoming radial, and PT-17 with the equivalent Continental. But their airframes are so strong that postwar operators, who used them extensively for crop dusting hung 450-horsepower Pratt and Whitney Wasp Jr.'s on many of them without a second thought, a tradition followed by many antiquers today.

The Boeing Model 75, the Kaydet, the PT-13, the Navy N2S—it's been called a lot of names. But to biplane lovers, it will always be Stearman.

Boeing Kaydets pulling up into a loop.

Boeing Model 75 Kaydet, universally known as THE Stearman, in civilian colors after a career of military training and crop dusting.

looked into the support that Continental had been giving it to sort out its teething problems, however, he became enthusiastic and authorized the airplane's development.

In the meantime the 90 had made a promising first flight and was undergoing an intensive flight test program. Lyle Farver, however, had left in mid-project because he felt he was getting too much interference in the design process from management. He was replaced as chief engineer by Fred Knapp, who, as we may recall, had quit on Don Luscombe at Monocoupe in the middle of the D-145 project because he felt he was getting too much interference in the design process from management. Don Luscombe's relationships with his associates were always mercurial, to say the least.

In addition to picking up the 90 project midstream, Knapp also took on the design of the small Luscombe, which was designated the 50 once the decision was made to go with the 50-horsepower engine. Don Luscombe requested that there be as much commonality between the two designs as possible to benefit from economies of scale in production. This goal was accomplished mostly on the fuselage of the two aircraft. From the cabin aft they were identical. Another novel feature to facilitate mass production was the empennage. On each type the vertical and horizontal stabilizers were interchangeable with only minor adjustments.

The wing was an all-metal skeleton structure with aluminum sheet covering the leading edge and fabric covering the completed panels. The wing inboard of the trailing edge had a sharp angular cut to join the fuselage at a straight section. This was a clever way of dispensing with the need for expensive fairings along the curved section of the fuselage where the wing would have otherwise joined it.

The control surfaces were scalloped on the production Luscombes. This technique, a fairly common practice on light aircraft even today, gave them sufficient rigidity without the need for formers and resulted in a lighter structure than the steel tube and fabric control surfaces of similar size.

The landing gear structure was simpler and the gear much better behaved than the one on the Phantom, but if there was an enduring criticism of the Model 50 it was that the wheelbase was too narrow, which could make landings squirrely, especially in a crosswind.

The Luscombe 50's first flight was in December 1937. When it returned to the field the company's employees felt

The Cessna 120/140 turned out to be what the Luscombe 8 should have been if management hadn't been distracted by office politics that saw Don Luscombe forced out of the company. The postwar 120/140 was very similar to the Luscombe 8 and more than 10,000 were built before being superseded by the Cessna 150 and 172. Pictured is a Cessna 140, which in 1997 was still running on its original engine (it had been stored in a barn in a dry place with 200 hours on it, so the new owner just cleaned it up when he bought it 20 years later and has been flying it ever since).

The Ercoupe was designed by Fred Weick, a former NACA engineer. It was radically different in appearance from its contemporaries, with tricycle gear and interconnected rudder and ailerons that made it impossible to spin the airplane. About 100 Ercoupes were produced before the war, followed by 6,000 when peace returned. The postwar recession affected its sales and no more were made; but quite a number of them are still about, and it is a much-liked antique today.

Private flying as envisioned by the optimists at the end of World War II started to become a reality in the 1950s. Investment banker Robert Schroder flew his Ercoupe on the weekends for a change of pace from the excitement of Wall Street. As the affluent society took off, so did recreational flying. Note the Luscombe in the background.

A whole new meaning to wingloading. Actually such photos were popular to demonstrate the strength of delicate-looking wings. Luscombe employees take a break on the sturdy Luscombe 8. *National Air and Space Museum*

as if they had received a Christmas present. It was an instant source of fascination with the aviation press and the flying public. Following the resolution of some minor problems, such as a tendency to experience carburetor ice, and some further tweaking of the airframe, it was certified in August 1938 as the Luscombe Model 8. It completely overshadowed the Luscombe 90 in sales, a revealing sign of the times. The 90 was only about 20 miles per hour faster than the Luscombe 8 in cruise, yet it cost $4,000 compared to $1,900 price of the 8.

Its modern metal construction had as much to do with the Luscombe 8's brisk sales as its performance and low cost. "No wood! No nails! No glue!" shrieked a company pamphlet. Today small metal cabin airplanes are the norm, but back then the Luscombe 8 was an exotic sight indeed. Demand was soon running at about 30 airplanes a month. The Luscombe 8 also compared favorably in performance to the J-3 Cub and the Aeronca Model B. With the same engine the Cub cruised at 80 miles per hour, the Luscombe 8 at 94 miles per hour. The Cub had a reach of about 250 miles, the Luscombe 360 miles. The Cub's useful load was 465 pounds, the Luscombe 8's was 550 pounds.

The Model 8's 50-horsepower A-50 was replaced within a year by the 60-horsepower A-65, which made it a really peppy airplane. It was called the Luscombe 8A. Thereafter Luscombe 8s appeared with a variety of increasingly powerful flat-four engines up to 90 horsepower. They were excellent performers in any version and sold well. By 1942, when the line shut down because of the war, about 1,200 Luscombe 8s had been built. This was not as high as the Cub and the Aeronca, which had much more extensive sales networks, but it certainly was mass production.

The most significant contribution to personal aviation was not the Luscombe 8's good looks, nor its performance, but its construction. Luscombes were much less labor intensive, and therefore less expensive to build than the traditional wood, fabric, and steel tube airplanes. The Luscombe 8 was the harbinger of the postwar modern mass production of light metal aircraft with which the traditionally built airplanes could no longer compete on a large scale. The army of Cherokees, Cessnas, Bonanzas, and others that would flood the market in the 1950s, 1960s, and 1970s by the tens of thousands would all be built essentially like the Luscombe 8.

Don Luscombe had his winner, but he wouldn't enjoy his accomplishment for long at the helm of the company. Luscombe Airplane was perennially short of cash. Money was so tight that Continental wasn't willing to ship engines on credit. To keep the company solvent Don Luscombe was forever wooing investors. As the Luscombe 8 was on its way to becoming a great success, he finally made one deal too many.

Leopold Klotz, a tough young German financier who had the good sense to be on the right side of the Atlantic as his fatherland plotted Armageddon, made a small initial investment in Luscombe and used it to mount a successful hostile takeover of the company. One casualty was its president, Don Luscombe. The super salesman who gave the golden age the Monocoupe, the Phantom, and the Luscombe 8 would never play another important role in aviation.

Klotz ran the Airplane Corporation Luscombe responsibly and with great competence, but fell victim to the postwar recession after moving the company to Texas. TEMCO bought the rights to the Luscombe 8, but it was the end of the line for the dapper little airplane. It was left to the Cessna 120 and 140 to realize the commercial success that by all rights should have been hers.

The manufacturers of light aircraft powered by small radial engines had to respond to the flat-four revolution as the fleet of Cubs, Aeroncas, Taylorcraft, and the Luscombes equipped with them were beginning to number in the thousands. There was little they could do except make an attempt to join it.

Monocoupe, Porterfield, and Rearwin all re-equipped existing models with flat-four engines, but not until the more powerful 65- to 90-horsepower versions that could handle their heftier airframes became available. Several of these airplanes were quite promising, and for the first time their pilots understood the term "forward visibility," but they appeared too late to make a big impact on the market in the time remaining to the war.

The Monocoupe 90-AF, introduced in 1941 with a 90-horsepowre Franklin engine, was a lovely airplane. The Rearwin Cloudster reappeared as the Ranger and later the Skyranger. Porterfield was quite successful for a time with its flat-four-powered models. But in the end, the days of these firms were numbered. None of them had the financial staying power to survive the postwar economic shakeout, the flood of war surplus light aircraft, and the onslaught of the new, more modern designs.

Among the large cabin-class airplanes only Stinson took up the flat-four challenge. Its entry into this segment of the market was the two- to three-place Stinson 105 Voyager, first flown in early 1939 and certified a few months later. Initially powered by a 50-horsepower Lycoming O-145, it was a high-wing airplane of conventional wood, fabric, and steel tube

ABOVE AND RIGHT: The Cub Coupe was Piper's answer to the Aeronca Chief and the Taylorcraft, both of which featured side-by-side seating. It was also Piper's first attempt at introducing a little automotive-style luxury into one of its airplanes.

construction. Its graceful, prosperous lines faintly resembled its large cabin-class Stinson heritage, but it also had links to Fairchild, for its development was overseen by Lewis Reisner, who formerly ran Fairchild's Kreider Reisner division.

A novel feature of the Voyager's airframe was the set of permanent slats on the wing's leading edge to reduce the onset of stall.

Safety was becoming as big an issue, as it is today. Given the less comprehensive understanding of aerodynamics back then, the spin was the great bugbear of the day. Stringent CAA regulations had to be met on spin tests by any new type, and Stinson set out to make the Voyager unspinnable. This was initially accomplished by restricting up elevator travel, but it then transpired that there wasn't enough elevator to properly control the flare. To solve the problem Stinson designed a crafty mechanism that linked the flaps and elevator and automatically increased elevator travel when the last notch of flaps was extended. It seems that good spin training would have been a simpler solution.

The 50-horsepower Lycoming on the prototype was woefully inadequate, but the Voyager wasn't even designed for it. It had been hastily installed only as an interim measure until the specified 75-horsepower Lycoming was ready. With the proper engine the Voyager was a delightfully downsized cabin-class Stinson. It cruised at 105 miles per hour, hence the Stinson 105 designation, and had a range of about 350 miles.

The Stinson Voyager benefited greatly from Stinson's wealthy clientele for its Reliants. Many of them thought of it as a little sports car and were eager to have one around as a local runabout. Actor Jimmy Stewart flew one until he traded up to the left seat of a U.S. Army Air Corps B-17 over Europe and a squadron command. Aviator Roscoe Turner and

Cub Coupe, period instrument panel. *National Air and Space Museum*

National Air and Space Museum

153

A New Lease on Life

Keeping antique airplanes alive requires a great deal of dedication, skills, and resources. Quite a few antiquers are talented restorers themselves, but many others rely on a small band of professional restorers such as Mark Grusauski. To visit Wingworks, the shop where Grusauski works his magic, is to step back into the 1930s.

You wind your way through a small Connecticut town onto a lonely country lane. As all signs of the present recede, the forest parts, and you come upon a small grass airfield set among the rolling hills. It is North Canaan Airport, home of Wingworks, where any airplane younger than a Luscombe would look out of place.

A bright yellow Cub and a Cessna 140 peer out of a row of sheds—and the 1929 Parks biplane that author Richard Bach once flew from the Atlantic to the Pacific, reliving the barnstormer's life and telling about it in his book *Biplane*. Behind the black Model A Ford is Grusauski's Wingworks hangar where ancient airplane carcasses are re-created into the Wacos, Howards, and Champs they once were.

The Wingworks logo.

Grusauski came by his skills the old-fashioned way, like Matty Laird, and Bruckner and Yunkin before him. He has hung around ragwing airplanes ever since he can remember and built a hang glider when still in high school. Cub and Champ restoration projects followed, and then bigger airplanes, and before he knew it he was a professional airplane restorer.

The lack of replacement parts is Grusauski's biggest challenge. Much of the restorer's finest work today is making new parts from scratch. Grusauski has all the machinery to fabricate anything that was part of an airplane going back to the Wright brothers. And if he has to, he'll get the airplane's blueprints from the Smithsonian's National Air and Space Museum.

Most of the raw materials the old wrecks need to be resurrected are readily available. Ceconite has replaced Grade A cotton, but the steel tubing, the plywood, and the aluminum sheets are the same. Grusauski also does his share of tracking down rumors of old parts and rare materials. His biggest find to date: a big stash of wood blocks in an old-timer's proverbial barn, stamped "Sitka Spruce—1932."

Some of that wood has become a new set of spars in a YKC-S Cabin Waco that was restored from the ground up and required most of the wings to be built from scratch. When the Waco was structurally completed, it was covered for a while in clear Mylar to allow people to see how these old airplanes were built. There isn't a more effective way to grasp at a glance the meaning of steel tube, wood, and fabric construction.

Besides the Cabin Waco, which was being finished up, restorations of a big-cabin Howard DGA and an open-cockpit F series Waco were under way recently. A lot of Grusauski's work goes into restoring and maintaining a growing collection being assembled at North Canaan by antique airplane buff Larry Smith. Pride of place in Smith's collection belongs to a sparkling Spartan Executive, one of seven still flying out of only 34 built. But the Spartan will be getting some competition from a pristine Staggerwing about to join the collection.

Grusauski wasn't even born when his personal Champ first took to the air. But like so many antiquers, there is nothing he'd rather do more than keep alive the heritage of the personal airplanes of the 1920s and 1930s by keeping them flying.

Mark Grusauski (right) and a colleague are working the pneumatic hammer to form the wheelpants of a Howard DGA. Beating metal stock into the desired complex forms is a lost art, but was a common technique for forming the few metal components of the aircraft of the 1930s. Metal stamping and design that avoided parts with compound curves gradually replaced custom hand forming.

Wood was a popular material for aircraft construction because it is light, easy to work with, and exceptionally strong if properly used. Here the plywood skins of a Howard DGA's wings are being restored. Plywood skinning was used on many higher performance aircraft of the 1930s because it provided a very light, rigid structure.

The fuselage of a Howard DGA restoration nears completion. Note the structural steel tube fuselage frame and the selective use of metal skinning. The rest of the fuselage will be covered in fabric.

Another lost art is the stitching of fabric to the wing's ribs, a technique that goes back to the earliest days of aircraft construction. Here a Cabin Waco's wings are nearing completion. Aircraft manufacturers in the 1920s and 1930s employed armies of seamstresses to perform this job.

Mark Grusauski with a Cabin Waco he restored and covered in Mylar temporarily to exhibit how aircraft were costructed in the 1930's.

The Mylar covered cabin Waco's fuselage graphically illustrates the most common fuselage construction technique of the Golden Age. The steel tube fuselage frame carries the structural loads. The wood formers support the fabric cover and are used to give the fuselage the desired aerodynamic shape.

The Cessna 140's panel is still in the mid-1930s mold. Note, however, the automotive-style GE radio.

OPPOSITE: The Cessna 120/140 assembly line churned out more than 10,000 aircraft in the years immediately after World War II. Monocoque construction techniques dramatically reduced construction time. *National Air and Space Museum*

wealthy businessman Howard Hughes also owned Voyagers. Approximately 2,200 of them were built before the war, and it was one of few prewar types that would be back when peace returned.

While Don Luscombe was engrossed in getting the Luscombe 90 and 50 into production and Stinson wooed its wealthy client base with the cute Voyager, a great bonanza was about to befall their competitors, Piper, Taylorcraft, and Aeronca, with far-reaching consequences for the future of personal aircraft. As is often the case in aviation, it again had to do with war.

The first big break was the Civilian Pilot Training Program, or CPTP for short. It was launched in the summer of 1939, in part as a public works administration project, but also in response to events in Europe. As war clouds gathered across the Atlantic and Lucky Lindy waxed poetic about the kinder, gentler side of the Nazis, more worldly minds were realizing that America was facing a world war with a disturbingly inadequate peacetime air force. Should war come, they reasoned, it would be useful to have a large pool of people with at least basic flying skills. The CPTP was their solution to closing the gap. Its main beneficiaries, besides the tens of thousands who learned to fly on the government (and the flying schools that

turned them out), were the manufacturers of the trainers equipped with the flat-four engine.

Largely fueled by the CPTP's needs, Piper sold 1,800 Cubs in 1939 and more than 6,000 in the next two years. Taylorcraft and Aeronca had a problem unheard of a few years before. They were now struggling not because they couldn't sell enough airplanes, but because they were having a hard time keeping up with demand. Their sales were now in the middle to high hundreds per year. There was even room for upstarts. A California company brought out the Cub-like Interstate Cadet and sold 200 of them for the CPTP.

Another great opportunity materialized for these manufacturers in 1941 when on military maneuvers in Tennessee the Air Corps was tasked with providing observation aircraft and ended up having to hastily borrow civilian airplanes to do the job. The maneuvers turned into highly successful field trials for Piper, Taylorcraft, and Aeronca as their airplanes proved to be the indispensable eyes of the ground troops. When a crusty old cavalry general called one a damn grasshopper, the name stuck, and the U.S. light liaison/air controller fleet of World War II was affectionately known as the Grasshopper Air Force.

The postwar Globe Swift was strongly influenced in design by Al Mooney's Culver Cadet. It was a hot ship, too hot to become a mass-market airplane. About 1,400 were produced, and it still has a loyal following of real pilots.

Taylorcraft and Aeronca brought out tandem versions to meet the military's requirements. The armed forces bought another 5,700 Piper Cubs (known as the L-4 in military parlance), 2,200 Taylorcraft (L3), and about as many Aeroncas (L2). Taylorcraft, which had set up a license manufacturing arrangement in England, also became a major builder of observation aircraft for the British armed forces. It supplied about 1,800 of its tandem airplanes, known as Austers, equipped with the British Cirrus Minor and Gypsy Major engines and the Lycoming O-290.

Luscombe lost out on the liaison contracts only because the military wanted tandem seating, and it would

have been a major project to redo the Model 8's high-tech metal fuselage. Stinson on the other hand was eventually successful in securing a place in the Grasshopper Air Force for its military derivative of the Voyager, which was designated the L5. With permanent leading-edge slats and a 175-horsepower Lycoming instead of the Voyager's 90-horsepower engine, its short field takeoff and landing profile was reminiscent of an elevator ride. It had an especially wide role in the Pacific and was affectionately dubbed the flying jeep.

Many of the airplanes equipped with flat-four engines that came out as the 1930s came to an end had

The Aeronca Champ is another classic favorite. Descended from Aeronca's L-3 military tandem two-seater, it was produced in the late 1940s by the thousands. The design survives today. It has evolved into the Super Decathlon, still being made, primarily for aerobatic instruction. The old-fashioned steel tube, wood, and fabric construction, with some stamped aluminum wing ribs thrown in, is still the most economical way to build them in very small production runs for niche markets.

National Air and Space Museum

airframes designed and built along conservative, established lines. The availability of the new, compact engines, however, also spurred other airplane makers besides Luscombe to create innovative airplanes that didn't reflect the past but offered a glimpse into the future. Among the more interesting examples of such designs were three diminutive low-wing airplanes that looked nothing like what came before them, the Culver Cadet, the Globe Swift, and the Ercoupe.

The Culver Cadet was Al Mooney's creation that went into production in 1940. It was a tiny low-wing, side-by-side, two-seat, wood-and-fabric airplane with retractable gear that achieved 120 miles per hour in cruise on a mere 75-horsepower Continental engine (an 80-horsepower Franklin-powered version was also available). The Cadet was an evolutionary step on Mooney's quest for the super-efficient, low-wing monoplane that had its roots in the Bullet he had designed for the Alexander Airplane Company.

The Bullet was not a success. It got four test pilots into unrecoverable spins, killing two of them. Mooney then designed an improved version on his own which he had no funding to produce. It evolved into the Monosport design, developed when Mooney was working at Monocoupe. The Monosport wasn't put in production either so Mooney moved on and joined forces with K. K. Culvert to build the airplane as the Dart, powered by 90-horsepower Lambert, Ken Royce (LeBlond), and Warner Scarab radials. It was a lively airplane, particularly noted for its aerobatic abilities.

About 50 Darts were built before the company switched to the smaller, flat-four-powered Cadet (and changed its name to Culver). The Cadet's time was numbered as a civilian airplane, but during the war it was modified for tricycle gear and went into mass production as a pilotless target drone. Some of these drones made fine inexpensive airplanes when after the war they were converted into piloted craft.

An airplane so similar in appearance and size to the Culver Cadet that it was undoubtedly strongly influenced by it was the Globe Swift. It received its ATC in 1942, too late to go into production, but is interesting because of its construction. Its wings and empennage were built from bakelite-bonded plywood. It was one of the first attempts to make a "plastic airplane," but with its original 65-horsepower Continental it was underpowered. The Swift returned after World War II, retaining its shape (and the Cadet's influence), but it was made out of metal and fabric and had a 125-horsepower engine. It ultimately didn't survive the postwar shakeout, but its fighter-like flying characteristics have attracted a passionate band of followers who keep quite a few of them flying today.

Perhaps the most unusual light aircraft to appear just before the war interrupted personal aviation was the Erco Ercoupe. Designed by Fred Weick, who had dedicated a good part of his career to research and development at NACA to advance aviation technology (among other achievements, he developed the NACA cowl for radial engines), it incorporated many features that were advanced for its time.

The Ercoupe was a low-wing all-metal airplane with fabric over part of the wings and a monocoque fuselage. It had side-by-side seating for two in a comfortable, enclosed cockpit. It was aimed at "everyman," as noises were beginning to be made about the approaching era of a plane in every garage.

To make it easy for "everyman," the Ercoupe incorporated numerous novel operating features. It had tricycle gear to take the mystery out of taxiing. With the yoke hooked up to the nose gear, on the ground the Ercoupe was simply steered as a car. It was impossible to spin the airplane. The rudder and the differential ailerons were interlinked through the yoke to prevent cross controlling (it had no rudder pedals), and in a steep bank the pilot would run out of 'up elevator' before the airplane could stall. On landing in a crosswind the technique was to touch down in a crabbed attitude. As the sturdy gear contacted the ground, the Ercoupe would weathervane into alignment with the runway.

The Ercoupe was powered by a 75-horsepower flat-four Continental, and it could scoot along at 105 miles per hour for 500 miles on a tank of gas. Any pilot who was technically forward thinking was bound to be attracted to it. Ultimately its unique control system was too intrusive on piloting skills to survive. Suitable for novices, it took away too much control from experienced pilots. Nevertheless it was a pleasant weekend

General Dwight Eisenhower in his L-4, the military J-3. The Grasshopper Air Force of J-3s, Taylorcraft, Aeroncas, and Stinson L-5s filled the battlefield liaison and forward air controller duties by the thousands. By Korea their role would be taken over by the helicopter and the Cessna Bird Dog.

flyer that has its diehard fans to this day. It opened the minds of many pilots to the possibility of alternatives beyond wood, fabric, steel tubing, and little wheels on the tail. Only about 100 Ercoupes were made before the war, but it would be back in force.

Thoughts about the future of personal aviation receded rapidly even from the minds of its most ardent practitioners as America became fully embroiled in World War II and faced an uncertain outcome. But as the war communiqués improved and victory became certain, the aircraft manufacturers turned their thoughts to postwar plans. Based on aviation's tumultuous wartime role and the fascination it generated in the public's mind, they forecast a tremendous increase in demand for personal aircraft. They envisioned servicemen returning by the tens of thousands flooding the nation's flight schools on the GI bill, and pretty soon there would, indeed, be an airplane in every garage.

Optimistic plans were laid to gear up for the postwar production of personal aircraft by the thousands. Old assembly lines were being dusted off, and new models were being derived from the interrupted prewar lines, all powered by the flat-four engines.

The Ercoupe was being prepared for the postwar boom. Aeronca developed the Champ with high hopes from its tandem military liaison airplane. Plans were laid to make the improved Globe Swift. The Luscombe line was being revived. Cessna feverishly developed the 120/140 which, some would say, was an outstanding updated copy of the Luscombe 8, except for the addition of the spring leaf landing gear (invented by the 1930s racing pilot Steve Wittman after whom Wittman Field in Oshkosh, Wisconsin, is named). North American, the maker of the T-6 Texan and the P-51 Mustang, had the Navion on the draw-

HOW TO FLY a PIPER CUB

MOVEMENT OF CONTROLS
AND THEIR EFFECT UPON ATTITUDE
OF THE PIPER CUB

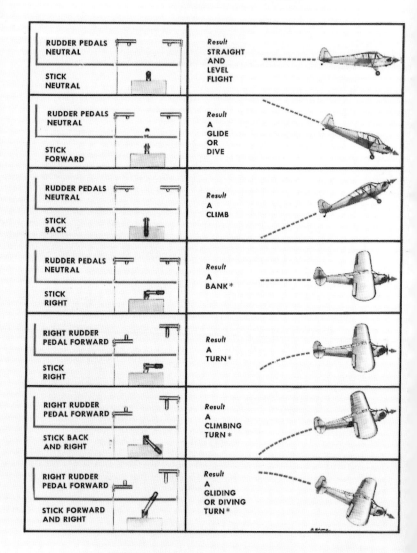

RUDDER PEDALS NEUTRAL / STICK NEUTRAL	Result STRAIGHT AND LEVEL FLIGHT
RUDDER PEDALS NEUTRAL / STICK FORWARD	Result A GLIDE OR DIVE
RUDDER PEDALS NEUTRAL / STICK BACK	Result A CLIMB
RUDDER PEDALS NEUTRAL / STICK RIGHT	Result A BANK*
RIGHT RUDDER PEDAL FORWARD / STICK RIGHT	Result A TURN*
RIGHT RUDDER PEDAL FORWARD / STICK BACK AND RIGHT	Result A CLIMBING TURN*
RIGHT RUDDER PEDAL FORWARD / STICK FORWARD AND RIGHT	Result A GLIDING OR DIVING TURN*

*These maneuvers are to the RIGHT. For maneuvers to the LEFT, reverse controls.

17

ing board. And Mr. Piper was standing by with all those Cubs.

Everyone was preparing for the unprecedented boom in personal aviation, and it was quite clear to most that the radial engines and the splendid machines they powered throughout those glorious roller coaster years of the 1920s and 1930s had their day.

The boom did come, but not without some rocky bumps while the economy readjusted from its wartime footing. When it really got under way, the big winners were those well-capitalized makers of inexpensive trainers who were ready within a few years for the affluent

society of the 1950s with shiny metal fleets of four- and six-seat touring airplanes—and Walter Beech won big again, this time with the Beechcraft Bonanza, a worthy heir to the magnificent Staggerwing.

But while the world of personal aviation swiftly moved beyond the Staggerwings, Reliants, and Travel Airs, the Wacos and Detroiters, the Stearmans, the Fairchilds and the Howards, the Spartans, the Monocoupes, and even the Cubs and their kin, they were by no means forgotten. Lovingly restored by people, young and old, who refuse to let them fade away in the name of progress, may they forever bring us a time when flying was larger than life.

First in their time. The Travel Air in the foreground was approaching the end of its line when this photo was taken in the late 1940s. Converted to a crop duster like so many of its peers, it gave no indication that it was once as hot on the line as the Beechcraft Bonanza with which it shares the ramp. Walter Beech's Bonanza was a worthy heir to the Travel Air's and the Staggerwing's reputation.
National Air and Space Museum

A page from Piper's *How to Fly a Piper Cub*, a booklet often given away free after the war to entice the public to take up flying. Initially the postwar economic readjustment kept personal flying below optimistically expected levels. But eventually tens of thousands learned to fly, many on the GI bill, leading to a boom in personal aviation that dwarfed anything going on in the 1920s and 1930s.

FOR FURTHER READING

There are many detailed histories on the different types of aircraft covered in this book that serve as important sources of information and would well serve the reader interested in further exploring the personal aircraft of the golden age.

Aeronca C-2: The Story of the Flying Bathtub, Spenser, Smithsonian Institution Press, 1978

Alexander Eaglerock, deVries, Wolfgang Publishers, 1994

Aviation Classics, Aviation Quarterly, 1984

Barnstormers and Speed Kings, O'Neil, The Epic of Flight Series, Time-Life Books, 1981

Beechcraft: Pursuit of Perfection, Phillips, Flying Books, 1992

Cessna: A Master's Expression, Phillips, Flying Books, 1996

Fairchild Aircraft: 1926-1987, Mitchell, Narkiewicz/Thompson, 1997

Mr. Piper and His Cubs, Iowa University Press, 1973 (also available from Flying Books)

The New Ryan, Cassagneres, Flying Books, 1995

Of Monocoupes and Men, Underwood, Flying Books

Ryan Broughams and Their Builders, Wagner, Aviation Heritage Books, 1991

The Spartan Story, Peek, Aviation Heritage Books, 1994

The Staggerwing, Phillips, Flying Books, 1996

The Stearman Guidebook, Mayborn and Bowers, Flying Enterprise Publications, 1973

The Stinsons, Underwood, Heritage Press, 1984

The Taylorcraft Story, Peek, Aviation Heritage Books, 1992

There Goes a Waco, Balmer and Davis, Little Otter Productions, 1992

Travel Air: A Photo History, Bissonette, Aviation Heritage Books, 1996

Travel Air: Wings over the Prairie, Phillips, Flying Books, 1994

U.S. Civil Aircraft Series, Volumes 1-9, Juptner, McGraw Hill, 1994

Visions of Luscombe, Zazas, Aviation Heritage Books, 1993

Waco: Symbol of Courage and Excellence, Vol. 1., Kobernuss, Heritage Books, 1992

Women Aloft, Moolman, The Epic of Flight Series, Time-Life Books, 1981

INDEX